GOD'S
DIRECTED
—PATHS—

by

R. Lloyd Black

God's Directed Paths

Trilogy Christian Publishers
A Wholly Owned Subsidiary of Trinity Broadcasting Network
2442 Michelle Drive Tustin, CA 92780

DEDICATION

to Pat

"Guid gear comes in sma' bulk." *(Translation: "Good things come in a small package.")*

—Scottish Quote

WHAT'S INSIDE

INTRODUCTION

In all your ways acknowledge Him, and He shall
direct your paths.

— Proverbs 3:6 (NKJV)

"I love to tell the story!
'Twill be my theme in glory
To tell the old, old story,
of Jesus and His love."

— C. Hankey (1834-1911)

I heard the old hymn, "I Love to Tell the Story" the very first time
that I visited my Grandpa's church. I was about six years old at that
time. My rare visit was for a special occasion: It was family reunion
day, but Grandpa would not dare allow any of the family members to
eat until we first had church.

Grandpa moderated the service, Grandma played the old foot organ, and I stared constantly at the old wooden instrument she was
frantically peddling. I wondered just how that skinny little lady could
demand such explosive sound from that old archaic musical box.

After a few minutes of Grandma's beautiful organ music, Grandpa
stepped to the front of the congregation. Then, he ordered everyone
in the house to stand and to worship Jesus. The few church member
present knew Grandpa expected them to participate. So, they all shuf-
fled to their feet almost simultaneously and pretended they were ready
to sing.

I felt a little uneasiness when he ordered all the children to come to
the front and to sing, but none of us grandkids tarried. All twelve of us
hurried to the front. Since I did not know the words to the song that

the church sang, I just moved my lips and pretended I did. I hoped that Grandpa would notice me.

Grandpa would interrupt the singing now and then and stir up the whole church to sing louder. Then, he would look over to we grandchildren and bellow out, "I can't hear you young'uns. Bessie," he'd say (that was Grandma's name), "Play it again. And you kids sing louder."

After we were worn out from a spell of extraneous singing, Grandpa preached until his face turned red. He never stopped, even when his old homemade clothes became soaked with perspiration. That day, Grandpa told the story about Jesus, and ever since that day, I have loved the story of Jesus.

Now, I want to tell my story. My story is about Jesus, also. Nothing more, nothing less, and nothing else. My story is about Jesus leading, feeding, caring, and shepherding me through more sixty plus years of ministry. Without Jesus, I have no story.

To tell my story, I needed a starting point. *But where do I start?* I asked myself. *And what is there about me that I would dare share with others? Let's see, I'm a husband, father, grandfather, great grandfather, pastor, author, former high school and college instructor, banjo strummer, guitar and bass guitar picker, bluegrass and country gospel wannabe singer; and for most of the time, a worry wart! But who really cares to know about that?*

To tell my story, I very soon realized that I needed more information about myself than I knew. *Just who is Raymond Lloyd Black?* I pondered. When I thought on that question, many other questions popped into my mind. *How did I encounter this journey with Jesus? Who chose my path of life: Jesus, or me?*

However, it was the final question that I asked myself which gave me the impetus to discover more about myself: *Why would God call a poor sharecropper's son to serve Him and then pour so many miracles into his long life of service?*

To answer the last question, I realized that I needed to talk to someone who was aware of my early years. I needed someone older than I. Just who could I get to introduce me to myself? It was then that I realized that I had outlived all those folks. *I'm the old-timer now,* I thought, shuddering. *I'm the last man standing!*

Then, I had a brilliant idea. *I will do an ancestry search and discover myself!* The thought of digging around my family roots began to excite me greatly. *There is no telling what I might shake out of my family tree,* I surmised, *if I can just find that special tree and give it tug or two.*

To get started on my family search adventure, I took not one, but two swabs from the old jaw. *Two DNA samples are better than one,* I reasoned. Wow! Was I in for a big surprise! I found out that I was Scottish, Irish, Scandinavian, French, German, Native American, and only God knows what else. After that bland ethnicity report was finally exhausted, I determined that I was a prodigy of all nations. However, I already knew that I was a really mixed-up person.

With my DNA report behind me, I was now ready to kick off my research project. I had already learned that I could not fly an airplane, ride a bucking horse, fix a computer, or play football. Now, I was about to find out that I couldn't negotiate the complex data bases that challenged my inquiry.

Sadly, I admitted that I was up to my neck in deep weeds. I spent more time digging around my family tree than I had ever spent on Facebook. To justify my long and tedious hard work, I told my wife, Pat, "I know I am important; I've just got to prove it."

Finally, with the aid of several genealogists, my ancestry research found solid footing, but before I turned those professional gurus loose, I set some boundaries and perimeters for their work. To illustrate those boundaries and perimeters, I told them a story about my childhood days.

The story centered around my twin brother and me when we were about ten years old. That was when my Daddy would take us rabbit hunting. Daddy most often chose to rabbit hunt on a very cold day just after a big snowstorm. The big snowstorm would more than likely pile layer after layer of clumps of snow on our harvested cotton stalks.

However, Daddy never bothered to take a shell for his old single-barreled Winchester 20-gage. He was too much of a conservatist to carry stuff like shells for his gun. He approached life's situations so pragmatically, and his conservative, pragmatic rabbit-hunting technique called for my brother and me to walk ahead of him and to kick every snow-covered cotton stalk.

Daddy told us that the rabbits claimed the white, snowy cotton stalks as monuments for their winter homes. He said that we boys needed to evict them. He said, "Just kick 'em up! They can't run away in that deep snow! Chase 'em down and put 'em in this tater sack, and just chase those you can catch, 'cause there's plenty to kick up!"

Looking back at those days of yesterday, I still shudder at the thoughts of those cold, frozen, and snow-covered cotton fields where my brother and me chased rabbits. Yes, sir. There were some really "good kicking" opportunities back in those days.

So, I instructed my genealogists to just "kick up" whatever could be easily found around my family tree. Furthermore, I told them to not go chasing every rabbit. I'm not sure they understood about the rabbit part.

With their help, I soon walked thousands of miles via internet. I flew hundreds of miles, professionally arranged by Google. I even garnered preferential treatment at the gates of old villages, grave sites, and courthouses, and with great delight, I viewed ancient black-and-white family photographs and archaic paintings. All in all, I think that I had a glorious homecoming. I felt greatly rewarded by my family search. I met relatives whom I had never known, and I gained a wealth of knowledge about my ancient family members who lived five hundred years earlier.

However, after four years of hard work, endless roadblocks, and dead-end streets, I finally put the genealogy project to bed. My four-year research project had taken the wind clean out of me. I'm sorry to

R. Lloyd Black

say that I did not find enough material about my forefathers to prove my importance, but I did discover two gems of greater importance. I discovered that many of my predecessors were pastors, preachers, teachers, and Bible-believers. No generation before me was without a family member who served the Lord Jesus Christ.

I also discovered that most of them had traveled down four common pathways during their lifetimes. Beginning in the 1500s and running all the way to the twentieth century, generation after generation shared the common pathways of *suffering, searching, serving,* and *sifting*.

When I unearthed this amazing fact, I looked within my own personal walk with God. I also realized that God had led me along those same four common pathways. So, this is my story. My story is about Jesus, who led both my ancestors and me on four common pathways.

In each of the four chapters present in my story, you will briefly meet one of my distinguished ancestors. After that, I will attempt to share insights about my relationship with my forefathers and my own personal walk with God. Then, you will be challenged to consider your own personal walk with God.

When I began to write my story, I was immediately reminded of my literary weaknesses. So, I placed two quotes before me. The quotes inspired me and encouraged me. Each is from a well-known literary genius.

Charles S. Spurgeon said, "God does not need your strength, He has enough of His own. He asks for your weakness," and William Faulkner said, "A story is in you. It just has to come out."

— R. Lloyd Black
Russellville, Arkansas
August 2020

THE PATHS OF
Suffering

In all your ways acknowledge Him, and He shall direct your paths.

— Proverbs 3:6 (NKJV)

T he Paths of Suffering" is a brief historical account of my predecessors who walked along God's directed paths of suffering during the days of their life on this earth. It also shares a short selfie of me and my own personal path of suffering.

Speaking of suffering, it reminds me of the horrible hour that we are presently facing with the COVID-19 virus. COVID-19 attempts to knock at everyone's door. It scares the living daylights out of the masses and it pulls at the nerve-strings of both the young and the old.

Warren Wiersbe said, "Our pleasure focuses upon outside opportunities; but our suffering is an inside job." Helen Keller wrote, "We all belong to the greatest company in the world; the company of those who suffer." My favorite one-liner from an unknown source says, "Suffering does to an individual what suffering finds in that individual."

PREDECESSORS SUFFERING

Suffering certainly found my predecessors to be tough cookies. However, they were determined to follow God regardless of pain. I found them on the path of suffering when I initially met them in my genealogical search.

My ancestors lived in Paris, France. Their French name was "La Noir" (French for "Black"). They were primarily sheep ranchers, but they were also very religious. They devoted their homes to the constant study of the Bible and to prayer. Because of the religious oaths they had publicly taken, they were called Huguenots. Huguenots means "oath-takers." They had publicly declared their belief that salvation is by grace through faith, and they had also taken an oath that they believed the Holy Spirit could interpret the Word of God without the need for the church's assistance.

As you may surmise, these tenants of faith were viewed by the Church as hostile acts.

Soon, all the Huguenots were publicly identified with the spiritual reformation that had engulfed Europe. The La Noirs had helped to lead the array of new spiritual thought in their hometown of Paris. It was easy to see that the La Noirs were deeply devoted to the preaching and the teaching of Martin Luther and John Calvin.

The Huguenots' religious preference eventually gave rise to both controversy and conflict with the state church, and on St. Bartholomew Day in the early 1500s, thousands of Huguenot believers were slaughtered while they sat in prayer and Bible study. Then, the remainder of the Huguenot sect was exiled to Africa, Germany, England, and Scotland. The La Noir (Black) family was among the believers who were banished to Scotland.

Scotland offered a peaceful and blissful setting for the people who had been on the road of suffering. The La Noirs readily joined the newly formed Presbyterian Church that flourished in the highlands of Scotland. The La Noirs were permitted to continue the practice of many of the Huguenots' teachings, and in the process of time, the La Noirs formally adopted the Scottish equivalency "Black" for their surname. Life was great. Peace invaded their lives, and the local church sang the old Scottish blessing, "Lang may yer lum reek," or, "We wish you well for the future." However, the Blacks soon discovered that they had not reached the end of their road of suffering.

A few years later, the Black family was ordered to uproot and reestablish their homes in neighboring Ireland. At the Port of Ulster, Ireland, the Black family was classified as "Ulster-Scots". The Ulster-Scott label basically expressed the idea, "While you may reside in Ireland, you can never be Irish." This social stigma hovered over the Black family for the rest of their days in Ireland.

In the early 1700s, John Black and his two brothers, Samuel and Anthony, left Ireland and sailed to America. Each of these three Scotsmen soon walked the bitter paths of suffering. John spent his wealth and health in his effort to develop Virginia both socially and religiously. Samuel had accepted the pastorate at the prestigious Brandywine Presbyterian Church in Pennsylvania. However, Rev. Black was forced to step down from his position, and Anthony was slain in the Revolutionary War.

When I read of their demise, I thought of the words of A. Judson: "There is no success without sacrifice. If you succeed without sacrifice, it is because someone else suffered before you. If you sacrifice without success, it is because someone will succeed after you."

Therefore, I would like to think that what little success that I have had in life has been attributed to the suffering and the sacrifice of someone before me. No doubt. My family who came before me certainly made it easier for me to journey along my own pathway.

Now, allow me to share with you some of the insights of my association of suffering.

ASSOCIATION WITH SUFFERING

When I look over my shoulder at the path of pain my ancestors trod, all my stories of suffering lose their morbid luster. My predecessors faced real pain, persecution, and severe problems. And me? Well, I mostly encountered disgust, disappointment, and unfulfilled desires, and it would be deceitful for me to imply that I was able to navigate around the omnibus path of suffering that stretched endlessly before me.

I suppose that my path of suffering initially began on the road of social and financial difficulties. At my birth, our entire nation grimaced with pain in its attempt to get back on its feet. It struggled to overcome the Great Depression. Soup lines announced the physical hunger in our land; furrowed brows boasted of the psychosocial paranoia that swept the land of the free. However, before the Great Depression could be defeated, this hungry and unemployed country called America was swept into wars with both Germany and Japan.

It was a time of hopeless and a national feeling of worthlessness. Too many Americans were unemployed, depressed, and suicidal. It was during that period of economical demise that my parents struggled immensely, but their struggle was consigned to the rural life. They were Arkansas sharecroppers. Their little twenty-acre share crop lay buried in the weeds and gumbo mud in western Woodruff County.

A share crop was socially and economical designed by the federal government to give poor families a place to live and a track of land to farm, but the wealthy landowners scooped up what profits that the share crop farm produced. It left the poor worker with nothing but a resolve to live and to work another day.

My Daddy and Momma struggled daily to prepare the soil, plant the seed, worked the plants, and harvest the few bolls of cotton that the little farm provided. They were always challenged by the unmerciful tree roots, briar patches, Johnson grass, crap grass, tree saplings, and hard gumbo soil for the land rights. Their expectations of a good life faced daily challenges. However, I believe that someway, somehow, they just leaned upon the Lord. Neither grumbled—nor complained. They just kept their wits, humor, enthusiasm, and determination to live the victorious life of the Arkansas sharecropper.

While the work on the little cotton farm was difficult, the living conditions posed even a greater headache. Clean water, electricity, educational opportunities, sanitation, personal hygiene, health, and safety benefits simply did not exist.

A small hand-pump in the backyard supplied the only source of water the sharecroppers could expect, and two small coal oil lanterns kept the little farmhouse lighted. Sharecroppers had an old saying: "No one here on the cotton farm is old nor sick, 'cause the old and sick have already died."

During the days of the sharecropper, suffering haunted each farm family. The curse of poverty and the lack of a good quality of life roosted like ugly vultures over the bedeviled little shanties. Someone said, "We live here, but we have no life here!"

———

It was during those social and financial difficulties that I was born. My birthday was shared with my twin brother, Floyd, but it was also shared with four mid-wives, a mother who had no idea she was giving birth to two boys, and a Daddy who was as nervous as an old fighting rooster.

My birth would have been completely ignored had it not been for a birth certificate and my twin. The old family doctor from Cotton Plant arrived on horseback much too late that hot June afternoon. He just scribbled some information on two birth certificates, cussed a blue streak, and spit tobacco juice on the small cotton stalks which grew around our porch, and rode away on a horse, muttering to himself. At birth, the mid-wives nicknamed my brother "Skinny Jack." They called me "Curley." Odd thing! Neither of us resemble those nicknames today.

A few years later, several of the neighbors said, "Those Black boys sure do look alike." I know for certain they were referencing our "soup bowl" haircuts, cut-off overalls, dirt beads around our necks, and the millions of freckles that had invaded our skinny, sun-burnt bodies. Our environmental similarities certainly make us look like two peas in a pod.

My brother and I soon garnered an exquisite fan club. We were even featured in an article in the county newspaper. The newspaper story was relative short, but it did make note of the happy life of a sharecropper, his wife, and their two little "cotton pickers." The story went viral in our small county, but to my knowledge, the article never did go global.

Until the day that I left home for college as a teenager, our house was never equipped with indoor plumbing, air conditioning, nor other modern conveniences. Times were definitely hard.

Even after all these years, there is never a day when I take a hot shower and I don't say, "Than You, Lord, for this good, hot running water."

My path of suffering may have been predicted when I was only four years old. On that that hot summer day, my brother and I celebrated our birthdays with a fresh coconut cake, eight very tall candles, and a few excited relatives. Even my grandfather, who was a minister, drove down from the city to share the special occasion.

After we had blown out the candles, Grandpa asked my brother and me what we planned to be when we grew older. I blurted out, "I'm going to be a preacher!" It frightened my brother, for sure, and it surprised even me, but hardly anyone else paid the remark any mind. Now, the "preacher" part may still be debatable, but the words I spoke that day about becoming a preacher pointed to God's directed path of suffering for my life. Of that, I am certain.

A few years later, on our seventh birthday, my teenage sister died from her long battle with rheumatic fever and heartaches from a marriage that had gone bad. As she lay dying on a small cot in the back of that little farm house, she reached upward and said, "Momma I have to go. They [the angels] have come for me. Look! They're everywhere!" And like that, she was gone.

I looked a long time that night at the ceiling where she saw the angels, but I never did see any angels. My heart was broken. I heard my Daddy cry for the first time in my life. I watched my Momma sob with great grief and sorrow.

I still remember some questions that I had during that dismal evening. *"Why did God take my sister away from us?"* *"Why did the little baby's father abandon her Momma and her?"* *"Does God enjoy taking one of our family members away from us?"* *"Why did he not answer our prayers that night when we prayed so hard with tears?"*

After I became a pastor, I stood hundreds of times in front yards, backyards, houses, mobile homes, hospitals, baby wards, jail cells, busy highways, cemeteries, and various other places just to talk to the grieved and broken-hearted people who had lost a loved one. I attempted to share answers to questions that were born out of their anger, disbelief, grief, and pain. I could always remember the night that my sister died. I never forgot my pain, sorrow, and disbelief.

I sincerely wanted to lift their burdens, answer their questions, and prepare them for the long, sad road that lay ahead. I never hurried in my attempt to comfort the bereaved. I knew personally the pain and agony of the death's billows and the dark waves of sorrow.

The night my sister passed, I had no preacher to come and to comfort me. Perhaps if one had been with us that dark night, he would have explained to us that Christians live on promises and not explanations.

My path of suffering grew more intense the summer my sister died, but God had a plan for my life. Little did I know that God had purposed to introduce me to old-fashioned Pentecostalism, healing and speaking in tongues through my period of suffering.

The summer my sister died, I grew quite ill, myself. The doctor dropped by, watched me for a while out of the corner of his eye, and told Momma that I would soon die, too. While he never examined me, he told her that he was sure I had the rheumatic fever, too.

It is not known for certain what brought on my severe illness, but my malady corresponded with the continuous spraying of insecticide on our cotton field. Redesigned World War II fighter planes were employed to deliver the poisonous chemical to our crops to kill the insects and boll weevils. The World War II pilots were called "crop dusters."

Consequently, for one reason or another, our milk cow, two working mules, dog, cat, chickens, and ducks mysteriously died, also. Then, my entire body was invaded by a virus that initiated large boils. My leg swelled. It was difficult to work in the cotton field. Momma had to reduce my diet to plain white rice and poached eggs, which the neighbor supplied. I was one sick boy.

However, just a couple of miles or so down the dusty road from our house was a little white-framed building. The building had a hand painted sign that read "Church of God." That summer, the pastor had called for prayer, fasting, and a week of revival meetings.

I'm not sure how Momma heard about the event, but the next thing I knew, she had me wrapped in a lightweight homemade quilt, lying in the bed of our wagon, and Daddy driving me to the revival meeting.

After the message that evening at the church, the evangelist called for those who wanted divine healing. I had no idea what divine healing was all about, but Momma quickly carried me down to the altar to meet the evangelist. The evangelist sat back in an old cane-bottom chair someone had placed for him. Then, he took me into his arms and placed both of his hands over my head and ears, and I heard the preacher talking in a language that I had never heard. I was very frightened in one way, but comforted in another. It was like a battle of two forces within my youthful head. I could sense that something mighty was about to happen.

Soon, the evangelist's clothes were soaked with perspiration, but he never stopped speaking in that unknown language. I felt my clothes being satiated with perspiration, also. God was doing a work on this sharecropper's boy. Then, after a long period of "speaking in tongues" and praying, the evangelist stood me upon on the floor in front of him. I discovered that God had completely healed me of the boils. In later years, no doctor could find a trace of the rheumatic fever. That night in that Pentecostal revival, God completely dried up my sicknesses

R. Lloyd Black

and diseases. He did it with the same Breath of Power that had earlier swept over the Red Sea.

I believe in the hour of my suffering and disease that God purposed to get me under the umbrella of His divine healing and power. Since the night of that revival meeting, I never fail to tell others that I was introduced to Pentecostalism through the spiritual gifts of healing and speaking in tongues (1 Corinthians 12, 14).

———

My path of suffering continued into my college days. God had blessed me with a job on the campus in my second year of study. It was difficult. I had to wash dishes three times a day in three wash tubs, and I also had to keep the dorm cleaned where I roomed, but I was delighted to be able to continue my college education.

Consequently, my life in the dormitory soon became a spectacle. Several of the boys wanted to know why I kept a ragged old Bible on my bunk bed. Others became furious when I refused to drink liquor or participate in the dorm parties. The "x" on my back was just too big for them to overlook. I became the victim for the "preacher and the prostitute" jokes, but the jokes suddenly turned to ridicule. Then, the ridicule turned violent. While three or four forced me to the floor, others attempted to force alcohol down my throat.

I determined that I could not go on this way. So, I decided to leave college. My nerves had snapped, my dreams had faded, and my anger welled up mightily inside me. I felt that God had abandoned me. I wanted so badly to turn my one-hundred-and-twenty-pound massive body into a lethal weapon. I could see the walls coming down just like in the story about Samson.

However, God never failed me. Soon, He leveled the playing field. That spring, the campus was struck with a deadly tornado. On that dreadful night, a mighty wind force ripped unmercifully at the dorm, and while the storm huffed and puffed, first one student and then others slipped into my room until my living space was completely filled.

When the lights finally came back on in the dorm, my small living space was filled with nervous students from wall to wall. Other boys were standing in my doorway, and behind them more boys were lined up down the hallway from my room. On my bed with his feet and legs pulled under his chin was Jackson. Jackson was the seven-foot tall, all state, all conference basketball player: the ringleader of those who taunted and tormented me. Jackson was crying!

That night when all was settled down and my room was deathly quiet, God spoke to my heart and said to my spirit, "For this reason, I have called you to comfort those who suffer in the storms of life."

I still hate liquor, beer, and any form of alcoholic beverage. The demonic spirits that ride upon those demented drinks almost drove me off God's directed path for my life.

I learned a great lesson during that time of turbulence in the dorm. I determined after that to make lifelong decisions based in convictions and not on emotions.

With college graduation behind me, I spent the next twelve years teaching high school, college, seminary courses, and completing various writing projects, but nothing kept me away for long from my pastoral assignments, and one of my pastoral assignment coincided with the nation's oil crises in the 1970s.

During that period of time, consumer finances were difficult to negotiate. Interest rates skyrocketed, and national unemployment reached an all-time high. Our entire world groaned for mercy and relief, and the little church that I was assigned to had its own problems. It was too weak to function financially, it struggled to offer any pastoral assistance, and it never had enough matured church members to initiate a hostile board meeting.

However, the church parsonage looked even worse. It looked more like a weekender for the deer hunters than it did for the preacher's family. When I saw the makings that I had to deal with, my feet kept wanting to just walk away. My head kept suggesting that I forget the pastoral work and get a decent job to feed and care for my family, but while I was having a pity party, my wife, Pat, was pulling our "stuff" off the U-Haul. She knew I was having second thoughts, and she also knew that God had sent us there to pastor.

Just like that, we moved into the penthouse—I mean, parsonage. Pat set up housekeeping. Then, we made ready to meet the saints at the church the following Sunday. I discovered that the move in the U-Haul had rubbed a large hole into the sleeve of my only suit coat. While I was surveying the damage to my suit coat, the phone rang. I was told, "Tomorrow at the church, you will be expected to preach the funeral of the 'mother of our church'!" *My, what good timing*, I thought.

The next day, I put on my "holy suit!" I walked with poise into that pulpit for the first time and led the celebration of the dead and gave hope for the living, but through it all, I made absolutely sure that I kept my arm down by my side at all times! It was an awkward sermon, for sure, but I had grown accustomed to preaching awkward sermons. I was good at that brand of sermonizing. The poor lady who was the "mother of the church" was given a beautiful and timely service, and no one ever knew that I had on my holy garments.

After the funeral that day, my mind panicked at the knowledge that I needed money for my little boy's heart surgery. My wife and I had known from his birth that surgery was eminent. I reasoned with God that I needed to look out for my son's surgery expenses, and what had God done? He had placed me with a congregation that was too poor to even buy band-aids.

However, the day after the funeral, a high school English teaching position was posted in the county newspaper. Since I had taught for several years both high school and college English classes, I felt pretty good about my chances of getting the position. Man, was I excited! I was ready to walk on water. I just knew God had changed His mind; He was going to finally help me, and I was equally surprised to learn that God had discovered my address. So, I immediately called the school office and asked for an interview.

When I arrived at the school office for the interview, I was told to go into the principal's office. The principal finally asked me his last question: "Mr. Black, just what brings you to our community?" I told him that I had just been appointed pastor for the church on "such-and-such" street, but I was not prepared for what was about to happen. The principal angrily interrupted me with a raised voice and said, "As long as I am principal of these county schools, no Pentecostal preacher will ever be employed here." *Oh! That stung!*

I was stunned, flabbergasted, and angered! I was also shocked to hear a professional community leader speak so hatefully and with such prejudice. I had a sudden urge to retaliate, and even thought of some choice words to lay heavily upon him, but I didn't say anything. *Thank God!* However, on the way out, I thought about the old Scottish phrase: "You are all bum and parsley." Translated, it means, "You are all mouth and trousers!"

I drove my old worn-out Ford Pinto off that school campus that day in disgust, disappointment, and disbelief, but I didn't go home. Instead, I made my way to the mountaintops above the town. I stopped when my car stopped. It was out of gas. I got out and walked to the edge of the road and look a way, way down. I could see plainly the large, zagged rock formation hundreds of feet below. Then, I heard for the first time in my life the voice of Satan! He said, "Why don't you just jump off? You're a loser. You are a failure. You can't even supply the needs of your family, and your church doesn't care anything about your financial needs."

That day on the top of that high mountain, I knew for certain that I was walking on God's directed path of bitter suffering for my life.

A few years passed. The hospital called. The message had come for my son to have his heart surgery. He needed to replace his damaged valve as soon as possible. I certainly was not ready for that.

During the heart procedure, I went to the hospital chapel to pray and to be alone. I was so angry with God. I felt that He had let me down. I had asked Him over and over again to heal my son. I told Him how faithful I had been. I told Him how I had kept my son on the altar, and I was disappointed that He had not done His part to heal my boy. "God, You are the one to blame," I cried.

In the prayer chapel that day, I am sorry to say, I allowed the devil to take me back to that night when my sister died of heart disease. I listened to Satan as he told me that my son had the same disease as my sister had had and that he would die as she did. In a matter of a few minutes, I became a real basket case. So, I cried. Then I cried again. Then I cried for a very long time. I must have cried through most of the hours of my son's surgery procedure.

However, God's grace broke my period of grief after a long season of crying and venting my anger. His grace came as majestically as the golden rays of sunbeams shine through dark and fearsome storm clouds. His compassionate Spirit fell on me in like many buckets of comforting grace. My self-pity party stopped immediately. In a few seconds, I heard God speak to my inner spirit: "Put your trust in Me, not in your son's heart. I can cause your son to live without a heart!"

When the surgery was completed, the surgeon told my family that it was hardly possible for my son to have lived with such an abnormal heart valve, but it was not the valve that had kept him alive; it was God's grace!

That was over twenty years ago. My son is now married today to his high school sweetheart. He is a business entrepreneur, and the father of two of my intelligent and beautiful grandchildren.

I learned a lot that day of surgery for my son, and one principle that I mastered was that when no road leads us away from the suffering God plans, God walks that bitter road with us.

THEOLOGY OF SUFFERING

God gave me four principles of suffering to consider when I walk the pathway of suffering:

I believe that God's directed path of suffering prepares me to share God's comfort with others.

who comforts us in all our tribulations that we may be able to comfort those who are in any trouble, with the comfort with which we ourselves are comforted by God.

— 2 Corinthians 1:4 (NKJV)

God always has a purpose in mind when He comforts me. "Comfort" here means "strength" and "to come alongside!" See also the book of John, chapters 14-16. In my own personal language, I often tell myself that God is walking alongside of me to comfort me in my suffering, but even in this simple analogy, I know that God has a purpose for my calamity. God comforts me so that I can comfort another when the opportunity presents itself. I am sorry to confess, but in the past, I have often acted like the two men on the road to Emmaus. I failed to recognize the Person who walked beside me. Instead of walking by faith, I often look for God's footprint, but I know that when I cannot see God's footprint, I can trust His heart.

This past year of 2020, my sister gave up her two married daughters in death. She and her husband struggled tremendously. I hurt for her, my dear brother-in-law, and the rest of her children. A few weeks ago, I preached the funeral of my twin brother's only daughter. She was the mother of two married children. Oh, how my brother hurt, and, oh, how I hurt to share a word of empathy.

However, I observed that it was a rare comfort for him to converse with my sister who had lost her two daughters. She knew just how to express her own hurt in words that I have never experienced. Her words carried weight, depth, and value because she carried in herself the same pain and sorrow, but in time, God comforted her, and she was able to render some comfort to my twin brother.

Someone once wrote, "Your greatest test comes when you are able to comfort others when you are facing your own personal storm."

I believe that God's directed path of suffering
teaches me to trust God and not myself.

> Yes, we had this sentence of death in ourselves, that
> we would not trust in ourselves but in God who
> raises the dead.
>
> — 2 Corinthians 1:9 (NKJV)

The Old Testament character, Abraham, helped me to learn this principle. It was when he was "as good as dead" (Hebrews 11:12) that God used him to beget a nation of kings and priests.

I want to further illustrate this principle with a short story I heard when I was about nineteen years old. That year, I was appointed state evangelist for our church affiliation. Shortly after my appointment, one of our local churches called me to lead a revival meeting.

On one of those mid-week meetings, my state overseer just so happened to drop in to worship with us. I was nervous as a cat on a hot tin roof. After the service had concluded that night, the church official asked to drive me home. Since I had no automobile of my own, I was thankful for the "lift," but I also pondered the purpose of his generous offer.

After a few gentle and kindly pleasantries on our way back to my house that evening, the overseer asked, "Do you mind, Brother Lloyd, if I tell you a story as we drive along?" I could not say "No," but I knew down deep that I had a subtle message coming my way. He started by saying, "Now, Brother Lloyd, there was a young preacher who had the 'stuff,' clothes to match, knowledge, diction, voice projection, and cologne to boot. He strode into the pulpit with the charge and the stamina of a Charlemagne. He was armed with the best homilies, illustrations, statistics, and recall of current quotes. He cited both the Greek and the Hebrew. He revealed his knowledge of Bible geography and history. But his sermon flopped. He left the pulpit like a Humpty Dumpty. As that young man walked down the side isle of that big city church, weeping bitterly, a saintly old lady gently took his arm and said, 'Young man, if you had entered the pulpit like you came out, you would have come out like you went in!'"

Needless to say, I got the message! Ever since that day, I seldom read this verse of scripture without my remembrance of that "lift back home" that night, for it was then that I learned from the wise elder of the church to trust God and not myself.

———

*I believe that God's directed path of suffering
provides opportunities for others to come alongside
me and to pray for me.*

you also helping together in prayer for us, that
thanks may be given by many persons on our behalf
for the gift granted to us through many.

— 2 Corinthians 1:11 (NKJV)

R. Lloyd Black

In 2 Corinthians 1:8-9, we learn that Paul is facing certain death, but the prayers of the church changed his fate. Instead of being handed the sentence of death, Paul received a give of life. He called the prayer a "gift granted." The two words in this verse, "helping together," give us the understanding of "working with and under." Many in the church were working with Paul and were under his leadership.

I believed that I have survived many years of sorrow and toil simply because of others. God never failed to surround me and my family with certain saints who worked tirelessly with me in this compassionate ministry. Others labored under the burden of intercessory prayer for me and for my family.

Early this morning, a dear saint of God in our church texted me to inquire of our needs. She wanted me to know that God prompted her to rise in the wee morning hours to pray for us and our family. She did not know (though God knew), but we needed the call, and we needed the prayer. This is a gift bestowed upon us.

So, I understand that when I suffer, God is up to something more than just comforting me. He is calling others into the prayer ministry to pray for me, and He is inviting others to bestow a spiritual gift of intercession upon me and my family.

I believe that God's directed path of suffering overcomes all adversities.

In the letter sent to the Corinthian church, the Apostle Paul names four specific types of suffering that he and his associates had experienced. However, with each of the sufferings that his team had encountered, Paul voices a victorious chant. Have you ever felt surrounded by your adversary, demoralized by situations, terrorized by fear, abandoned by the Lord, or cast aside as a piece of worthlessness? Read this:

We've been surrounded and battered by troubles, but

we're not demoralized; we're not sure what to do, but
we know that God knows what to do; we've been
spiritually terrorized, but God hasn't left our side;
we've been thrown down, but we haven't broken.

— 2 Corinthians 4:8-9 (MSG)

I know beyond a shadow of a doubt that God is still in the game
with me and my family. God is not only in the game with us; He is
leading our fight.

Now, I am trying to live the rest of my life in light of the testimony
that Paul shares in 2 Corinthians 4:16-18:

> So we're not giving up. How could we! Even though
> on the outside it often looks like things are falling
> apart on us, on the inside, where God is making
> new life, not a day goes by without his unfolding
> grace. These hard times are small potatoes compared
> to the coming good times, the lavish celebration
> prepared for us. There's far more here than meets
> the eye. The things we see now are here today, gone
> tomorrow. But the things we can't see now will last
> forever.
>
> — 2 Corinthians 4:16-18 (MSG)

"Although the world is full of suffering, it is also full
of overcoming suffering."

— H. Keller

R. Lloyd Black

I mentioned earlier that we cannot see God's footprint in our day-by-day path of suffering, but we can always trust His heart, because God is good and God provides the best for His own.

I also wrote earlier about members of my family who had encountered bitter suffering along their way on God's pathway, but I was able to read the rest of their stories. Then, I saw how the hand of God was leading them even in their troubled times.

Reverend Doctor Samuel Black, who had received his doctorate from the famed Edinburg, Scotland Theological Seminary, and whom I introduced earlier, had a happy ending to his life. He had been charged earlier with drinking, neglecting his pastoral duties, and preaching faulty doctrine by a disgruntled sect within his congregation. However, within a few weeks, he was fully exonerated. He was asked to resume his ministry, but Dr. Black quickly declined. Instead, he traveled southward to Virginia to meet up with his brother John. During the following years, the two brothers won hundreds of poor Scots, Irish, and German immigrants to the Lord and built Presbyterian houses of worship. Then, they opened Christian schools and Bible training camps throughout the poverty-stricken region. The path of suffering led Samuel to his richest harvest field.

In the church town where the school principal spoke so harshly to me, miracles began to happen. Both myself and my church walked in the abundancy of God's graces and gifts.

Later that afternoon, after the principal had talked so rudely to me, Pat asked me how the interview went. I did not disclose all the morbid details; I just wanted to shelter my wife from the horrible manner in which I had been treated by the principal. So, I said, "Today, God told me we were going to be the most successful church in this town." Of course, God did not tell me that! I just spoke it by faith.

Within three years, our church reached an all-time high for attendance. Our building was completely full on Sunday mornings. We enrolled one hundred plus children in our new daycare. When one of the community churches closed its Christian Academy, I jumped at the opportunity to persuade the staff and student body to come to my church—free of rent. Many of the doctors, lawyers, and other professional people in the city had children in that group who came. Our finances increased. The church purchased a nice brick parsonage. It later paved the church parking lot. I started a Christian counseling class for a dozen pastors who also served other denominational churches in the county. I completed my lab work requirements for my seminary doctoral studies. I wrote my doctoral thesis. I later published it under the title, "Practical Pastoral Principles for the Small Rural Church."

However, the greatest thing of all was that I discovered I was not the loser the devil said I was that day on that mountain. God had a plan and a purpose for me. It just took God's path of suffering to get me where I was supposed to be.

Sometimes the storms that we encounter in life are not to destroy us. God uses them to clear our path for the rest of our journey.

SUMMARY AND APPLICATION

An old Irish proverb says, "Life isn't about waiting for the storm to pass, but about learning to dance in the rain."

To summarize my path of suffering, let me share two lessons that I have learned:

- I learned that Jesus never attempted to explain suffering; He just experienced it, and His example of suffering and resurrection from the dead proves that suffering cannot defeat us. He had one solitary source of strength to help

Him bear his suffering in this life:

> fixing our eyes on Jesus, the author and perfecter of
> faith, who for the joy set before Him endured the
> cross, despising the shame, and has sat down at the
> right hand of the throne of God.
>
> — Hebrews 12:2 (NASB 1995)

- I learned that we do not live on explanations. We live on
  the promises of God. Someone told me that the Bible
  has three hundred and sixty-five promises. I believe that
  is a promise from God for each day of our year. However,
  I learned that when we have Jesus as our personal Savior,
  we can have all the promises at one time.

> For all the promises of God in Him are Yes, and in
> Him Amen, to the glory of God through us.
>
> — 2 Corinthians 1:20 (NKJV)

Now that you have read my story about suffering, why not consider
your own pathway of suffering?

- What are some lessons or principles that the Lord has
  taught you in your period of suffering? Can you find the
  rationale that Paul used for his suffering in his writings?
  Carefully study the entirety of 2 Corinthians chapter 4.

- What biblical reference would you share if someone
  asked you to explain the reason God allows you to suffer?
  Look back in Genesis and read what Joseph said about

his era of suffering in chapter 45.

• What did the writer have in mind when he shared Hebrews 5:7-8?

• Suppose you could recall, add, and present in a ledger the total of all your suffering! How would it compare with Paul's evaluation of his suffering? See 2 Corinthians 4:7-10.

THE PATHS OF
Searching

In all your ways acknowledge Him, And He shall
direct your paths.

— Proverbs 3:6 (NKJV)

T he Paths of Searching" offers short stories about my predecessors and myself as we searched along God's directed paths.
When I think about my ancestors, I'm reminded of a quote
from Mark Twain: "Why waste your money and time looking up your
family tree? Just go into politics and your opponent will do it for you."
However, I never got involved with politics. So, I had to spend time,
money, and a lot of sleepless nights searching for insights about them,
and I'm glad I did. I found stories that were worth both my time and
energy.

For example, here is a brief story cast in the early 1700s about John
Black and his two brothers, Samuel and Anthony—we met them earlier. These three brothers wanted to abandon the good and comfortable
life in Ireland that their father had provided for them. They chose to
sail to the frontier land of America to search for their fortunes.

PREDECESSORS SEARCHING

John, Samuel, and Anthony were the sons of the wealthy, prestigious
and influential sheep industrialist named James Black of Dublin, Ireland. James had made his financial mark in the hierarchy of Ireland's
wealthy people even though he was a Scotsman.

Since John was the eldest of James' three sons, his natural and ancestral rights provided for him a goodly portion of his father's legacy, but the spirit of searching gripped his mind and soul. While he was single, set for life, and situated in a winning financial scenario, his emotions could not be abated. He longed for the unknown. He searched for the uncertain. So, enthusiastically, John asked for his father's blessings, the company of his two younger brothers, and transportation credentials to make their one-way voyage to the new land called America.

John and brothers reached America in the early 1700s. John had packed very little in his water-stained duffle bags, Samuel had brought mostly books and papers from his seminary studies in Edinburg, Scotland, and Anthony had filled his few traveling bags with primitive news items about the war between England and the newly formed colonies in America.

However, it was the personal items that John brought to America that filled me with joy. John had purposely packed his father's family Bible into his leathery traveling bags. The Bible was a gift from his father James. It contained his father's name and a simple, scantly historical sketch of the Black family tree. When I discovered my name arrived in America in a Bible in the 1700s with my Scottish ancestors, I was overwhelmed. I thought of the promise recorded in Psalms that says, "Your word is a lamp to my feet, and a light to my path" (Psalms 119:105, NKJV).

I believe that the Word of God directed my forefathers in their search for God's directed paths. I know that the Bible has directed my pathway.

Since John was my sixth great-grandfather, I marked his appearance in America with a suitcase in one hand and a Bible in the other.

I spent a great deal of time studying the life and the work of John, much of which I could not include in this study. However, I would like to have counselled with him. I would have asked him about the Bible. Perhaps he used it to lighten the new pathway in America. I discovered that he was eventually buried in Indiana. He is mentioned in the early history of that Indiana town as the oldest Scottish family member to settle in that portion of the midwestern state.

I also learned that the Bible that he brought to America with my family name in it is thought to rest in the archives in the same city where John is buried.

ASSOCIATION WITH SEARCHING

Like my forefathers, I searched along God's pathway to find meaning and purpose for my life. My search for meaning and purpose actually began as a surprise to me. Allow me to explain.

I was surprised to learn about an outburst that I had made when I was in my third grade classroom. I shared the classroom with a dozen or more other boys and girls. There were an equal amount of fourth graders who were also assembled with us in that same little smelly classroom. The teacher who taught both the third and fourth grades was Mrs. Butler. Mrs. Butler was a saintly lady. When she was not teaching school, she was helping with the ministry at the Methodist church in our cotton community. She was definitely loved by all of her students.

Both the third and the fourth grade classes met in the two-story building that was constructed by the W.P.A. workers during the Great Depression era. The McClelland Elementary School was certainly a noisy, but happy group of students in the late 1940s.

Mrs. Butler generally led both classes in a discussion each Friday afternoon. That is, providing both classes had behaved "proper and mannerly" during the week of classes!

On this particular Friday afternoon, she chose for discussion "the probability of a voyage to the moon." I had heard about the moon, but I didn't know enough about the moon to launch any space talks. So, I just listened. Several of the students chirped right into the exchange. They offered great insights and opinions. Since it was the year of 1949 and NASA and the moon walk had not yet occurred, there were some excellent ideas and imaginations that filled the classroom that day.

Around twenty-five years after that moon discussion in the third grade, I was mowing the lawn at the church where I pastored. I watched a long, sleek black automobile drive onto the parking lot. As I made my way to the car, I wondered, *Just who could that be?* The passenger side window rolled down. A skinny arm motioned for me to come to that side, and the years could not hide the sweet face of the lady who had had such a great influence upon me. It was Mrs. Butler. She said she had heard that I pastored in the area and drove by just to say hello. We talked, we cried, and she said, "Before I go, I want you to know that I always knew that you would be a preacher!" Then, she recounted the story about my standing up in my seat the day we discussed the voyage to the moon. She said I spoke to both of classes with great conviction, saying, "God will not let us go to the moon because He is coming soon to rapture the church away." I was totally surprised to hear the story. I did not remember the "sermon" at all, and I was embarrassed to learn about the adamant position that I had taken on the subject!

After Mrs. Butler's automobile vanished out of site, I felt both delighted and honored that she came to see me. I was surprised at her personal assessment of me when I was only nine years old, but I regretted that I failed to tell her that I had had many sermons after that one in the third grade that also had faulty premises.

However, I was heartened to learn that at the age of nine, I believed in the imminent return of Jesus Christ to rapture the church. Somewhere and some way, I had searched out and found the promise that Jesus was coming back to earth again.

––––––––––––

I read a quote from S. Aurobindo that caused me to pause and to ponder my search for God's hidden meanings for my life. The quote reads:

R. Lloyd Black

"Everyone has in him something divine. Something his own, a chance of perfection, and strength which God offers him to take or refuse. The task is to find it, develop it, and use it."

Only God knows if I had anything divine within me in those days, but I know for certain that what I have accomplished for God is all His doing. God chose me, God's grace helped me, and God's power did the work of grace within me.

It was during those early years at the age nine or ten years old that I began to search along God's pathway more earnestly. My search led me to an old-fashioned revival at the McClelland Church of God. I was fortunate to have been able to attend the week-long services in that little wood-framed building. It was the same church that my mother had taken me to once before so that the evangelist could pray for my sickness.

Now, I was too young to understand the sermons that the ministers shouted out to us each evening, but there was plenty of Holy Ghost power to go around in that meeting as I recall. When the Spirit began moving and people began shouting, I began fearing. I liked what I saw, but I saw what I didn't understand, and what I did not understand sure did make me nervous.

As soon as the minister gave the altar call, I was the first responder, and throughout that entire week, I was a "constant seeker." I am sure that I encouraged the evangelist each evening. I was always the first to go. Sometimes I was the only one to go, but I never failed to go.

After I reached the altar, I had no idea on how to pray. I did not know even know what to pray, but I felt that I had overcome a great hurdle by going to the altar. The preacher told me to repent, but I did not know what "repent" meant. So, I just ducked my head between my knees and kept still and quiet.

Looking back at that revival and at the trips to that old wooden altar, I know that I was searching for the pathway of God. While I am not sure what I found in that altar, I am positive that it gave me some of the steps that I needed to take on my pathway with God.

Just a year later, my search to know God and to find His pathway for my life led me to an old, abandoned railroad track. The railroad track was at the edge of our cotton community. It was within a short walking distance from my house. The train service had been discontinued because the cotton acreages had been cut. There was no longer a need for a train to carry the bales of cotton to some faraway shipyard. Since there was no demand for the railroad track, I secretly adopted it for my place to walk and to talk with God.

I can remember clearly some of the events that transpired within me while I walked and talked with God on the old railroad track. I imagined that I was one of the "Holy Ghost evangelists" who had visited our church during that summer revival. Not only did I recall his profile, but I attempted to gesture certain movements that the ministers had made. Quite often, I would holler out trite phrases that I had heard them say. I probably looked a little weird waving my arms and talking loudly, but no one could hear me for a country mile. To this day, I often wondered if I frightened the little lizards that scampered before me on those hot railroad beds.

A couple of years later, my path of searching led me to the banks of Bear Slough where the pastor of the Church of God had chosen to build a brush arbor.

The pastor told the church that the community needed a miracle, and the miracle was needed to break up the dry skies. All of the farmers and sharecroppers needed a rain desperately on their drought-stricken cotton crops, which had lain seething in the torrents of heat and humidity.

So, the pastor told the congregation that the Lord told him to build a brush arbor and to pray until it rained. I did not know what the preacher meant when he said that the Lord talked to him, but the farmers did not seem to be bothered about the comment.

Then, the pastor encouraged his flock to prepare to fast and pray.

Now, I did not know much about all that fasting and praying, either. I certainly did not know anything about the brush arbor he had said God told him to build, but I was overjoyed to see that the people believed his words and had begun to build a brush arbor. I saw my Daddy take on some encouragement, too. He didn't go to church, but he sure was sold on the idea that the church was going to pray for his twenty-acre cotton crop. Even Momma began to talk a little kinder. My brother and I noticed that she did not hit us near as hard with the stick of stove wood she kept handy to beat us in line.

Within a day or so, the church community had practically completed the brush arbor. Branches from the willow trees that grew along Bear Slough were gathered and fashioned into a structure. Fresh-cut willow bows with leaves attached were crudely placed on top for a temporary heat resistant roof. Room was provided for the vast numbers of extension cords, speaker cords, loudspeakers, microphone, guitars, tambourines, and the old, discolored accordion. Someone had even brought a wooden apple box filled with paper fans from the local funeral home, a bottle of stale olive oil, and two hand-pumped mosquito sprayers. One old farmer with a team of mules had taken it upon himself to haul a fresh load of sweet-smelling sawdust. He piled it deep and wide. No one moved it, so it just became the mourner's bench right where the old farmer pitched the shavings.

At last, the arbor was constructed, and the farm families were urged to come and pray. Each night there were singing, testifying of miracles, and praying until the people were too tired to continue. I always sat up front, but I kept an eye out to see if it was going to rain. I wondered why the preacher did not bring an umbrella, but now I know that umbrellas came much later to that cotton community. The preacher was too poor to have one, anyway.

However, it soon appeared that the wrath of the sun god had been evoked instead of the heavens being opened for rain. Days after days of horrible heat continued. The heat had a mind of its own and was bent on taking out the last of the struggling cotton plants. A few of the saints began to murmur and complain. "Why has God taken so long?" They asked, but the church kept on praying night in and night out. The theme song for the brush arbor meeting was, "Send down the rain, Lord. Send down the rain, Lord. Send down the latter rain." I still remember how we opened each service singing that course. Then, during the daytime, we added that little verse to our prayers. I even hummed it while I pecked at the dry clods of dirt in our cotton field.

On the third week of continuous praying, the rains finally fell from heaven in a mighty deluge. The downpour crushed the brush arbor and stopped the prayer meeting but defeated the heat wave. No one seemed to mind. Victory had been won. Prayers had broken the brazen heavens. New life had come to the cotton fields, the farmers, and the people in the church.

I was an eyewitness to the miracle of prayer. God had positioned me to witness the miracle as I searched along primitive pathways to know Him.

About fifteen years later, in a brand-new modern brick church with all the fancies, I was celebrating my new ministry and our new church building. However, one Sunday morning, the deacon informed me that the funds were short and the current mortgage payment could not be met. My first thoughts centered around the old Scottish saying, *Tatties o'wer the side*, which means, "Disaster has struck!"

After service had been completed that morning, I went immediately to my office and began to pray. When I began to pray, my mind went back to the day when the heavens were brazened, and our prayers were not answered. I prayed some more and then reflected upon the three weeks of bombarding heaven with an urgent request to send down the rain. Then, I told God that I needed "a God Miracle, just like the one that I saw in that old brush arbor."

I don't know how long that I prayed that day. I do know that I prayed until church time that evening. It was the first time that I really had gotten down to busing and praying in tongues for quite a spell. I do not know the interpretation of my praying that afternoon, but God knew. Little did I know that day while I was praying in the unknown tongues that I was about to experience a God miracle.

That night, the deacon told the church that a stranger had come by and said, "We do not attend your church, but God told us today to give an offering for the new building." It was a wonderful sum. I don't have to tell you, but that evening we had a grand ole, glorious, Holy Ghost, tongue-speaking, downpouring, outpouring, foot-stomping, devil-chasing, Satan-rebuking, healing, cleansing, revival camp-meeting church service, and our church never had to deal with the "shortage crises" again. Even our finance stream that fed our church ministries was opened that evening.

<hr>

Allow me to go back to the year that I turned eighteen years old. That year, I received the baptism of the Holy Spirit and spoke in tongues. I always considered the baptism of the Spirit was the crisis act of God in my life that defined my search to know Him.

I shared the story of my baptism in the Spirit in a book entitled Holy Ghost and Speaking with Tongues, which was written and published in 1983.

The gift from God was so profound and powerful that I made several lifelong changes. I changed my major in college from agriculture to journalism and English. I openly confessed my call to preach. I no longer wanted to suppress the announcement of my call, and I adopted the passage of Scripture found in Proverbs 3:5-11 and Matthew 6:33 as my philosophy of ministerial intent. I then vowed to walk in the light of God's Word to the best of my knowledge and ability as the light from heaven shined upon my pathway.

THEOLOGY OF SEARCHING

One of the most frequently asked question that I hear comes from young people. The question is, "How can I know the will of God's purpose for my life?" I will usually ask them to allow me to share the source of information that I used to know the will of God for my life.

My Guide to Know the Will of God:
Proverbs 3:5-10

My guide to know the will of God in my life is based upon Proverbs 3:5-10. I am not sure how I came to adopt the passage as my defining discipline for life, but I chose it early in life, and I determined to use it as my model, standard, and guide for the rest of my life as I walked on God's directed pathway.

I started very early in my life with a determination to trust the Lord. See verse 5. As a youth, I knew early that I had to trust the Lord for my future, because as a sharecropper's son, I knew that without God, I had no future.

However, to trust God wholly was very difficult for me. It was hard because my thoughts and mind were so full of doubt, unbelief, self-imposed barriers of poor self-esteem, and poor self-image.

It was a chore to start my trust in the Lord when I had grown so comfortable with my trust in faulty opinions about biblical truths, my dependance in family traditions, stupid fables, myriads of superstitions, etc.

So, trust was a task to master at first. I remembered too well about the times and the ways that I had watched my Daddy place his trust in others; because he could neither read nor write, he was taken advantage of by too many people too many times, and I hurt for him. Besides, I hated those whom he placed his trust in and who violated his trust. So, I struggled with the trust issue at first, but in time, with God's help and grace, I began to trust God more and more.

I wish I could say that I never failed to trust God later, but that would be untrue. However, I can say that I am much better with the "trust" part now than I used to be. I now have examples of God's faithfulness at work in my life, and I have seen just how reliable He has been in meeting my needs. I watched Him heal my family and meet our financial needs when we were in great need.

I wish I could have known earlier the story of Abraham and his growth in trust and faith. When God started with Abraham, the Lord required small steps of trust and faith. Then, after a period of time and testing, God gave to Abraham the ultimate test. You remember. God asked Abraham to sacrifice his son, Isaac.

Looking back over my life, God also led me a great distance before He required me to sign the dotted line of my ultimate trust in Him.

When I determined to trust God, I found that His idea of trust got a little demanding. I soon discovered that He wanted me to trust Him in all of my ways. See verse 6. I knew right away that I was in real trouble with that part of trust. I had a lot of ways that were not spiritual; I was constantly confessing doubts, fears, and sicknesses, and worst of all, I claimed daily the curse of poverty upon me and my future.

I must have said that I am "barely getting by" more times than I said my name. When I was asked how I was fairing, I quickly responded, "Fine, since I'm living under such severe circumstances!"

However, when I begin to trust the Lord in all my ways, I felt condemned for such talk and set forth to clean up my language, and God blessed the day I confessed that I was "living above the circumstances" and not "under the circumstances!"

On my journey to know the will of God for my life, God had to tell me two time to not be "wise in my own eyes" (verse 7) nor "lean on my own understanding" (verse 5). Sorry to say, I still have to watch my mouth, attitude, and actions about those two verses.

Since I had lived all of my youth with no health insurance except what the public school provided, I adopted verse 8 as my health insurance policy. Most theologians relegate this verse to mean "spiritual sickness" or some other metaphorical jargon, but I claimed the promise for my physical, financial, mental, and spiritual health. It worked for me. It made a difference in my body, mind, soul, and finances.

Then, I claimed verse 9 as my financial protector. Verse 9 says to honor the Lord with your possessions. When Pat and I opened our new home and our new lives together, we promised each other and God that we would give ten percent of our increase to God's "local church" without failure. We never considered our work in the church nor our offerings for various church-related projects to be counted for our tithe. We paid our tithes off our increase. Next, we gave offerings to the best of our ability. Our offerings were always above and beyond our ten percent tithes.

On various occasions I have been asked "Do I pay tithes on the gross or on the net?" I try to answer that question with another question! "Do you want God's blessing based on the net or the gross?"

It seems that all my years in service to the Lord has come to a full circle as written in verse 10. God promised Pat and me full barns and full wine presses. That promise has certainly come to pass in our lives and in our home. Our house is full. Our garage is full. Our automobiles' trunks and tanks are full. Our storage rooms are full. Our closets are full—I'm sure you get the picture! If we buy anything new, we automatically have to take something out of the house to make room for it. We are completely "full up!"

Besides the cluster of verses in Proverbs 3:5-10, I leaned very heavily upon the Word of Jesus as written in Matthew 6:33.

I was eighteen years old when I adopted Matthew 6:33 as both my landmark and my lighthouse. The verse served as my landmark because it marked the place and my purpose for my journey, and the verse served as my lighthouse because it kept me focused on my voyage in life. I now confess that I live in the abundancy of God. My saucer is full because my cup has overflowed!

I would like to conclude this portion of this chapter with an old hymn written by George Keith and a verse from the book of Psalms.

The old song is entitled, "How Firm A Foundation Ye Saints of the Lord." It talks about God's hand of protection upon those who search for Him on their journey in life:

> "When through the deep waters I've called you to go
> The rivers of sorrows shall not overflow
> For I will be with you your trials to bless
> And sanctify to you your deepest distress
>
> When through the fiery trials your pathways shall lie
> My grace all sufficing shall be your supply
> The flames shall not hurt you, I only design
> Your dross to consume and your gold to refine."

— George Keith

The Psalms describes how God leads us to the rightful place:

They wondered in the wilderness in a desolate way;

They found no city to dwell in. Hungry and thirsty,
Their soul fainted in them. Then they cried out to
the Lord in their trouble, And He delivered them
out of their distresses. And he led them forth by the
right way, that they might go to a city for a dwelling
place.

— Psalms 107:4-7 (NKJV)

HAND OF GOD

The hand of God has played a dominant role in my life since the early beginning. I believe that He has led me forth by the right way and that He is now leading me homeward.

It was the hand of God that played the major role in the most important decision of my life. While I seldom talked about my future with others or confided in others about my secret dreams, I definitely wore God's ear out. I kept the phone busy in heaven. I was forever asking Him to lead me and to direct me. My prayer life then was similar to that of Jimmy's. His prayer life was something like this: "Hello, God. This is Jimmy. Gimme, gimme, gimme!"

A lot of my prayers were about my goals in life. I was forever asking God to help me to get another semester of college, to finish college, to get an English teaching contract, to get a church to pastor, and to find and marry "Miss Perfect." While I never talked about my special lady, I often dreamed about her. I painted a portrait in my spirit for God to see so He could be better able to find whom I was seeking.

In Genesis 24, I discovered how Abraham sent his servant to a foreign land to "fetch" his son Isaac a wife. After I read about Abraham's success in finding a wife for his son, I begin to pray earnestly that God would do the same for me. It was a simple prayer, and it went something like this: "God, in the name of Jesus, just send the Holy Spirit to find me a wife just like Abraham's servant did." I told God that the person that He found for me had to be willing to accept me as a Pentecostal preacher and that she had to have the Holy Spirit baptism. Now, I knew Abraham, and I certainly knew that I was no Abraham, but I heard God had no favorites. So, I just kept on praying my "Abrahamic wife-fetching prayer."

During the summer months after I had completed my first two years of junior college, I worked hard at the little grocery store where I been employed for a number of years. I had also conducted revivals and made a few extra dollars. I had saved just enough money to enroll for one semester at the big state university about eighty miles away from my house. It was also the same summer that my pastor asked me to attend my very first Church of God state convention. The convention was being conducted in the same city where I had planned to enroll that fall in college. I didn't know it, but I was about to be introduced to more than the big college and my first state convention.

My pastor loaned me his black shoestring necktie and his white sports coat. I thought that I looked as fit as a fiddle. Then, the two of us were off to the big tent in the big city where the big university was. However, a bigger surprise awaited me.

While I don't remember anything about the Church of God convention program, I do remember hearing an unexpectant request that came from the back of the convention building. "Let Pat Chandler sing," someone yelled out!

Then I imitated all the heads that turned and watched a slender five-foot two-inch tall petite blond make her way to the platform. She grasped the only open microphone. I admit that I don't remember the title of Pat's song, but I still remember the feeling that came over me at my first sight of her. It reminded me of the old Scottish poem written by Robert Burns:

"Not the bee upon the blossom
In the pride of the sunny noon,
Not the little sporting fairy,
All beneath the simmer moon,
Not the poet in the moment
Fairey lightens in his e'e
Kens the pleasure
Feels the rapture
That thy presence gi'es me."

Of course, I was too bashful to even attempt to meet Pat that day, but I did quiz my pastor on the way home about her. I wanted to be deceitful, act naive, and not tip my hand about my feelings, but he was too perceptive for me to play my game. He caught my drift at the giddy up. I laid the white sport coat in the back seat, removed the long black string tie that had begun to choke me, and prayed that he did not see the big drops of perspiration that had popped out on my freckled forehead. There was nothing else that I could do at this point but to settle back in the seat of the big Pontiac. I knew that my pastor was about to provide me with a full disclosure of the blond-haired preacher's daughter.

On our two-hour drive back home, my pastor told me that he had known Pat for most of her life. He was careful to tell me that she had always been faithful in her local church. He even told me that she and her father had begun a mission work in a new field. "And oh, yes," the pastor said, "She is a member of the church and is filled with the baptism of the Holy Ghost."

Then, he grinned from ear to ear and spoke through his pursed lips, "Brother Lloyd, Pat is everything that you are not!" I soon found out what that meant. Pat was wired for 220. Her battery never needed charging. She never ran down, and through the six decades of marriage, she has had to jumpstart me, fix my flat tires, and give me a power boost just to keep my engine running.

R. Lloyd Black

Two years later, on July 26, 1963, Pat and I were married at the Arkansas state convention. She has since been the perfect wife for this preacher for six decades. She was my greatest discovery on God's directed path. She carried our family through all our bad times, but she never whimpered. She should have knocked me in the head many times; especially when I grumbled, talked negatively, and had to be dragged to church!

SUMMARY AND APPLICATION

To summarize my path of searching, I will admit that I did not have that defining moment that John Black had when he brought the Bible and the Black family name to America in 1700, but I do believe that my search for God's directed path defined just who I am today.

I liked what R. Brault said: "Never mind searching for who you are, search for the person you aspire to be." I certainly aspired to be just what God wanted me to be.

Perhaps William Faulkner had said the same thing earlier: "Don't try to be better than your predecessors. Try to be better than yourself."

There has never been an instance where I read the old poem, "The Road Less Traveled," which was written by the old Scottish poet, Robert Frost, when my own Scottish blood pressure fails to rise.

> "Two roads diverged in a yellow wood,
> And sorry I could not travel both.
> And be one traveler, long I stood.
> I looked down one as far as I could,
> To where it bent in the undergrowth.
> Then took the other, as just as fair,
> And having perhaps the better claim
> Because it was grassy and wanted to wear.

Though as for that the passing there,
Had worn them really about the same.
And both that morning equally lay,
In leaves no step had trodden black.
Oh, I kept the first for another day!
Yet knowing how way leads on to way,
I doubted if I should ever come back.
I shall be telling this with a sigh,
Somewhere ages and ages hence.
Two roads diverged in a wood and I—
I took the one less traveled by,
And that has made all the difference."

I searched for the path less traveled, but it was God's directed path for my life.

———————

- After you read my account of my search to find my way on God's pathway, what would you say about your experiences to know God?

- In the section "Theology of Searching," I shared that I adopted Proverbs 3:5-10 and Matthew 5:33 as sources of authority to direct my decisions in life. Do you have a similar biblical reference that you have come to rely upon? Write it here:

- What is one personal story that you recall that talks about your searching for truth, or answers, or for divine directions? Read Paul's account of his search as recorded in the book of Galatians, chapter 1.

R. Lloyd Black

THE PATHS OF
Serving

In all your ways acknowledge Him, and He shall
direct your paths.

Proverbs 3:5 (NKJV

PREDECESSORS SERVING

In "The Paths of Serving," I will share brief insights about my predecessors' distinguished service in the kingdom of God. Then, I will reflect upon God's directed path of service for my life.

Laban Calvin Black was my grandfather. He served as circuit rider for the Methodist churches. The handful of congregations that he attended stretched along the vast plains in Fannin County, Texas. He was a music teacher.

Laban owned little. Perhaps the horse he rode, the double saddle bags packed with old Charles Wesley hymns, and his oversized winter coat substantiated his wealth.

However, I am sure that Laban felt enriched by the love, the compassion, and the call of Jesus Christ upon his life.

In the winter of 1903, Laban finished his last musical session at the last church on that late night of multiple choir engagements. Little did he know that he had just made his last circuit ride. Within a few hours, Laban was dead. He had fallen fatally ill to the complications of pneumonia. His trench coat had failed to shelter him from the frigid cold wind on his ride back home that fateful evening. Laban was barely twenty years of age.

Laban's young teenage wife quickly turned her attention to her infant son. He was only a few months old. The baby would inherit nothing from his father but this brief story. Laban's son, Raymond Calvin, was my father, and my father loved to share this story. He talked about it as though it were his story. It was the only story that he knew, and his story always included the same bit of information about the path that his father walked to serve God.

———————

Several miles away and a few decades prior in the bluegrass state of Kentucky, a little dark-complexioned boy named Solomon Johnson Nichols was born. His mother had died shortly after his birth. Solomon's father felt that he would be unable to properly care for his infant son without the boy's mother to assist him. Consequently, Solomon was placed into the permanent care of the neighbor and his godly wife.

Within a few years, young Solomon made his confession of faith in the Methodist church. He immediately began a ministry as a circuit rider. He rode, preached, and taught the gospel of good news to several of the rural churches in the unsettled communities of Kentucky. At thirty-two years of age, he was ordained and appointed pastor. Then, he served in that capacity for sixty-two years. Solomon Johnson Nichols was my great, great-grandfather.

Solomon's daughter, Minerva Ann, beautifully modeled the Native American blood line of her mother. As a youthful teenager, Minerva Ann married a civil war soldier who just returned home from the bitter war. The soldier's name was Andrew Hunt Mitchell. Minerva Ann and Andrew Hunt Mitchell chose to spend the rest of their lives to care and to share the gospel in the Methodist church.

One of their sons, Marvin Monroe, followed his parent's footsteps into the ministry. Over the next sixty-plus years, Marvin planted numerous rural Nazarene churches among the poor and uneducated communities in Arkansas and Missouri. Marvin Monroe Mitchell was my grandfather.

What I have just shared with you brings both joy and gratefulness to me. I am ecstatic to learn about the paths of service that my forefathers walked.

I am aware that names like Laban Calvin Black, Solomon Johnson Nichols, Andrew Hunt, Minerva Ann Mitchell, and Marvin Monroe Mitchell were scarcely known in the days they served the Lord, but I believe that God led them on specific pathways.

I am reminded of a quote from Sally Koch. She said, "Great opportunities to help others seldom come. But small ones surround us every day."

My ancestors seized the small opportunities that surrounded them. They eagerly embraced those possibilities. Then, with the grace and the power of God, they poured the rest of their lives into the service of the Lord.

ASSOCIATION IN SERVICE

I would like to have known about my Christian legacy before I began my ministry sixty-plus years ago, but I didn't. Their stories surfaced abruptly only after I had begun my genealogy search.

Perhaps my knowledge of their stories could have given me inspiration, courage, and direction in my earlier days. Who knows? I may have even become a Methodist minister. However, I did not know their stories earlier, and I did not become a Methodist minister. Instead, I became a Pentecostal preacher.

Like my forefathers, my pathway of service was certainly unheralded. As a matter of fact, I did not even know that it had begun, but looking back over the years, I believe there were four distinct characteristics that marked my path of service for the Lord Jesus Christ.

God led me in 1.) preparing for my walk, 2.) planting seed for my harvest, 3.) producing fruit from my labor, and 4.) protecting the harvest that He gave me.

Preparing for my Walk

You might say that my preparation for my ministry was quite early. Actually, I was only four years old, for it was that year that I saved my first soul, and the soul that I saved was my twin brother's. In case you are wondering how I saved my brother's soul, it all developed around a big, deep, and black hole in our backyard. The dangerous pit was full of stagnant and murky water. Daddy had ordered my brother and me many times to "stay away from that big, deep, and black hole!"

However, one certain hot summer day when Daddy and Momma were in the cotton field, we two four-year-old adventurers were determined to solve the mystery of the big, deep, black hole in our backyard.

My brother reached the site of the mysterious place few seconds before I did, and like a flash, his foot slipped. Then, into the murky abyss he plunged. Seconds later, only his head could be seen above the brackish quagmire.

Somehow, by the grace of God, I was able to grab him by the hair of his head, and with God's amazing grace, I dragged him safely out of his miry pit.

Perhaps it was just a coincidence that happened that day at the big hole, but I believe God had foreshadowed my directed path of service, because I would eventually spend the rest of my life pursuing and rescuing the perishing and caring for the dying.

My preparation for the ministry also began naturally. By naturally, I mean that it began on a small cotton farm. The small cotton farm was Daddy's twenty-acre sharecrop.

Daddy's little twenty-acre sharecrop provided me with nature's finest laboratory, and this fine laboratory not only offered me opportunities to learn both the rudiments and the philosophy of plant and animal life, but it also gave me ample knowledge of the theory and practicum of seed time and harvest.

Theory and practicum began early each spring, because spring was the time of the year when you could find my Daddy breaking up the fallow ground. Breaking up the fallow ground was necessary before the seed for the harvest could be put into the ground for the fall harvest.

You could always find me walking behind my Daddy, his two mules and the one-row middle buster as he prepared the soil for planting. The middle buster that Daddy used was just an old rusty plough, but the plough was specifically designed to penetrate the soil's hard pan in our cotton field. The hard pan had to be penetrated, broken, and even crushed to allow the moisture in the ground to surface during the hot summer days to refresh the tender cotton plants. The hard pan was called "gumbo." Gumbo dried slowly when wet, hardened like cement, and stuck to farm implements like a tick on a dog's ear.

When my family and I worked the fields, we generally left our shoes at the end of the cotton rows each day at the close of our work. It was easier to allow the next rain to wash the gumbo away than it was for us to scrape them clean ourselves.

On one occasion, after a big rain had maddened the gumbo, I saw a twenty-five-pound soft-shelled turtle exhaustibly drag itself into our back yard. Its four feet had accumulated pounds of that gumbo stuff. I noticed that the turtle had managed to cement its gumbo covered feet against its rigid shell. The old guy was just plumb tuckered out! When I bent over to free its feet from the stick soil, I heard it say, "I think that I have gone the last mile of the way."

'Course, that's just an old turtle tale.

As I followed behind my dad and his middle buster, I cherished the aroma that came from the freshly-turned soil. The new earth soothed my calloused feet. It was a pediatrist specialty.

I filled my large coffee can with the fat red worms that the plough unearthed. Those creepy critters were used to catch the catfish in Bear Slough nearby. All I had to do was to place a big glob of worms on my hook, wave the wiggly creatures over the shallow water, and watch the big catfish walk right out of the water and grab my hook.

'Course, that's just an old fish story that I made up.

In my memories, I can still see by Daddy preparing the soil for the harvest. He knew exactly how to break up the "fallow ground" (Hosea 10:12). He just pointed the tip of the plough into the sod and removed all the roots, briars, and brambles that would hinder the seed from sprouting and growing. Daddy never allowed his harvest to be negatively affected by "stuff that doesn't belong," he would tell me.

It looked easy to me when I watched him long years ago, but the skinny little man with worn-out overalls and run-over brogan shoes labored far beyond his physical ability. However, Daddy was doing more than preparing the soil. He was also teaching the little boy who followed along behind him how to prepare the soil for a future spiritual harvest.

My season of preparation began early and naturally, but it also began without orthodox. My body had never been dipped in the Jordan River, nor my head anointed with vials of perfume from the Basham Valley, and I never discovered any hot oil in the palm of my hands. I never saw angels, nor the Shekinah glory of God. I knew nothing about oral, textual, source criticism, systematics theology, hermeneutics or homiletics, cross references, or oral tradition.

Neither Daddy nor Momma were "church-goers" when I was a boy at home. They practiced social distancing a century ago. No pastor ever dropped by our house to visit us, to pray for our needs, to eat a Sunday meal, to lead a Bible study, or to encourage us to come to church. We had no family Bible on our coffee table. 'Course, we didn't have a coffee table either!

On occasions, I heard Oral Roberts speak on our battery-operated radio. Oral said, "Put your hand on the radio as a point of contact." I had no idea what he meant by a "point of contact," but when no was looking, I put my hand on the radio just like Oral had said. I never felt anything, but it never hurt me.

A few days later, I saw my Daddy lay his hand on the radio, also. I'm sure he was listening to Oral. Daddy had developed a bad skin cancer on his forehead that was caused by the hot sun's rays. He did not know that I watched him, but I heard him tell my Momma a few weeks later that the cancer was gone. I always believed God healed Daddy the day he touched the radio and Oral prayed.

Then, one day I read the story about the prophet Amos. I grew immediately encouraged. I discovered how Amos had introduced himself. He said that he was not the son of a prophet, but just a farmer. I liked what he said. I saw right away that I was a lot like Amos. I thought that if God could prepare Amos to preach, then God could prepare me to preach, too. I marked Amos 7:14 (NHEB), where it reads, "Then Amos answered Amaziah, I was no prophet, neither was I a prophet's son; but I was a herdsman and a farmer of sycamore figs…"

No, sir. I was no theologian. I was just one of the sons of an Arkansas sharecropper who neither read nor wrote and who refused to attend church, but God had His own way to prepare me for my walk on His directed path of service.

Lastly, my season of preparation to walk on God's path of service began ever so imaginatively. When I was a boy, I had the greatest ability to imagine myself as a Pentecostal preacher and to incorporate my rural environment into my church setting.

Recently, I re-read the poem written by Patrick Kavanagh. His poem served as a spade to unearth some old memories, and the imagery of his work evoked childish fantasies of my preparation and walk with God.

Here is what Kavanagh penned in his poem entitled, "Canal Walk Bank:"

"Leafy-with-love banks and the green waters of the

canal

Pouring redemption for me, that I do

The will of God, wallow in the habitual, the banal,

Grow with nature again as before I grew.

The bright stick trapped, the breeze adding a third

Party to the couple kissing in an old seat,

And a bird gathering material for the nest for the
    Word

Eloquently new and abandoned to its delirious beat.

O unworn world enrapture me, encapture me in a
    web

O fabulous grass and eternal voices by a beech,

Feed the gaping need of my senses, give me ad lib

To pray unselfconsciously with overflowing speech

For this soul needs to be honored with a new dress
    woven

From blue and green things and arguments that
    cannot be proven."

You can readily see that Kavanagh's poem is cast with the Irish culture in mind, but the characterization of natural surroundings in the poem reminded me of Bear Slough. While I never walked on Canal Walk Bank, I did stroll on the banks of Bear Slough.

Bear Slough was just a little stream of water that ran quietly and lazily at the edge of our cotton field. In the springtime, it flooded, and at flood-stage, it appeared broad and impressive—sometimes scary! However, in the summer months, it dried to a few pitiful puddles. For the most part, it was the home to various species of small fish, mud cat, and numerous water moccasins.

I loved to walk along the banks of Bear Slough because my walks were often rewarded with natural surprises. Some days, I'd find a nest full of baby rabbits, and on other days, I might discover a scantly-covered nest of speckled killdeer eggs. Bear Slough was also the home to thousands of colorful monarch butterflies that danced like fairies on the beautiful wild buttercups and wild black-eyed Susans.

The rabbits, birds, and butterflies enjoyed the dense, unorganized, wild grasses, thorny shrubs, Johnson grass, sumac bushes, cattails, and dense moss that grew near the water's edges. Along with the animals, birds, flowers, and butterflies stood the emboldened and ominous cypress trees. They grew majestically in the shallow, stagnant water. Each tree expressed its own subtle mystique. I made a pole-raft once. I wanted to float near the picturesque cypress knees that grew around the massive trunks of the saintly trees. I pretended to be Huck Finn. However, the pole-raft sank. I did not know it then, but I had discovered the first Jurassic Park.

One summer day, the massive canvass and arcade of colorful grasses, cypress trees, and dewberry bushes enticed me to construct my own private hideout. I used my private hideout to say my private prayers. My prayers were short and my prayers were simple, but they always included the request for God to call me to preach, to give me special words to say, and to anoint me with the Holy Spirit. I know now that I had patterned my prayers after the evangelist who prayed for me the night God healed me. I could not forget him, nor the sound in my ears of his speaking in an unknown tongue. I could imagine myself being anointed someday with the Holy Spirit, speaking in tongues, and praying for the sick just like the evangelist had done for me.

I loved to pray in my secret prayer closet. I treasured the trees, the grasses, and the creatures that lived on Bear Slough, but my favorite attraction was the big "stage performance" conducted each spring on Bear Slough by the beautiful eastern cardinal. I called the magnificent creature the "Red Bird," and the Red Bird was my first theology teacher. The banks of Bear Slough were my first seminary classroom. On the banks, I sat with no laptop computer, lexicon, or linguistic thesaurus. Instead, I held in one hand a homemade fishing pole and a ragged straw hat in the other hand, and from the end of that fishing pole, I observed the Red Bird as it played out its role on God's natural stage of serving the Lord.

The Red Bird started with nothing. It chose its building material wisely, and then, with the decisiveness of a master craftsman, the brilliant red feathery creature constructed its home. It fashioned its dwelling with the tenacity of strength to withstand the spring storms and the fiery summer heat.

Today, when I pause to remember the Red Bird, I am reminded of the parable of Jesus:

> "These words I speak to you are not incidental additions to your life, homeowner improvements to your standard of living. They are foundational words, words to build a life on. If you work these words into your life, you are like a smart carpenter who built his house on solid rock. Rain poured down, the river flooded, a tornado hit—but nothing moved that house. It was fixed to the rock.
> "But if you just use my words in Bible studies and don't work them into our life, you are like a stupid carpenter who built his house on the sandy beach. When a storm rolled in and the waves came up, it collapsed like a house of cards."
>
> — Matthew 7:24-27 (MSG)

In my doctoral thesis, "Practical Pastoral Principles," I provided a simple theology of service for the young pastor of a rural church. The thesis was later published in the summer of 1977 under a different title. I reviewed what I had written about the minister's preparation in that publication. Would you believe it? In the introductory chapter of my thesis, I addressed the importance of both the pastor's call and preparation.

Now, you can rest at ease that I will not rehash the content of that earlier book, but I would like to refresh your memory of the "Red Bird" lesson that learned on Bear Slough. Like the little Red Bird in my childhood days, I also started with nothing, but I did not let the lack of nothing hinder me. I was determined to build a strong house. I chose carefully the best building material that I could find, and with God's help, I built my house to stand the storms of lies, deceit, criticism, controversy, jealousy, hatred, animosity, and hell's worst traps, mines, and pits that had been levied and placed against my family and me.

My home took on Satan's greatest hits and attacks, but my household withstood every test. My home was built on the Rock, and that Rock is Christ.

> They all ate and drank identical food and drink,
> meals provided daily by God. They drank from the
> Rock, God's fountain for them that stayed with them
> wherever they were. And the Rock was Christ.
>
> — 1 Corinthians 10:3-4 (MSG)

Planting Seed for my Harvest

I asked the pastor at the McClelland Church of God to allow me to start a Sunday school class. I was only twelve. I was usually the only young person who attended with any degree of regularity, but sometimes I would go to church and no one else came. My brother often walked to church with me. We had several miles to walk. Sometimes our path led us through flooded fields and sloughs. We often walked foot logs to church. The foot logs were cut by my Daddy and neighbors to enable the children to walk to school during the week. I was always glad when my brother walked to church with me. As a matter of fact, I was often too scared to walk to church by myself.

"I believe," I told the pastor, "I can persuade some of the other fellows to come to my class if you will appoint me Sunday school teacher!" And just like that, the pastor granted my request.

I invited my brother, the pastor's three mean boys, and three other close friends. While none of my Sunday school class ever became seminary teachers, worldwide evangelists, or television celebrities, three did surface later in my life. One served as best man at my wedding, and two of the pastor's mean boys became pastors. One still leads a church and keeps in touch, and the other retired recently after a long period of pastoral services. Consequentially, the latter is my grandchildren's other grandfather.

A few years later, I turned fifteen. I moved away from the sharecrop cotton farm and the familiar sights along Bear Slough. It would be my final farewell.

I moved a few miles down White River to a small river town. I got a job at the grocery store, where I would work until I left to teach high school. Next, I settled into the new school to complete my last three years of high school.

The weekend that I moved to the new town, I located the Pentecostal church. It taught the same way that the McClelland Church of God did. It was only a "mission" or "new field work," but it had a building that was not much more than a shale of a structure. It had hand-me-down homemade benches, but it looked like a cathedral to me.

The church was also small in attendance. We had a dozen or more who came when there was nothing else left for them to do.

I asked the young pastor to use me some way in the church work if he believed the Lord would be pleased. To my surprise, he appointed me Sunday school superintendent, and for the next three years I worked hard to build up the Sunday school attendance.

The pastor helped me to prepare for the ministry without me really knowing what he was doing. He called me his assistant. I helped with the serving of communion, washing the saint's feet, baptizing the

R. Lloyd Black

converts, and making house and hospital visits. He even invited me to assist with funerals and weddings. I also got to help with the yard work and the church cleaning.

God was preparing me for my walk on His pathway of service.

The summer I turned eighteen, I graduated from high school. I began to attend a house-to-house prayer meeting. Each evening I observed many poor, non-church people as they attended. Some were healed. Others were converted, and many of them were filled with the Holy Spirit. I wanted the baptism of the Spirit and to speak in tongues so very much, but it seemed that I faced a mountain when I tried to pray and receive.

Then, one night, several unchurched men laid their hands on me and prayed for me to receive the Gift. As they prayed, I begin to speak in an unknown tongue. Someone said that I spoke nonstop in tongues for almost three hours.

A few weeks after I had been baptized in the Holy Ghost, I had a dream. In my dream, I stood on the bank of a mighty ocean. The ocean looked like a crystal sea in one sense, but in another sense, it appeared to be a sea of people. The sea of people was so vast that I could not see the boundaries on either side, nor its depth. It was greater than my eye could see—especially looking forward. Some gentleman in my dream who appeared to be an official stood by my side. I knew that he was the officer in charge of the meeting. I also knew that I had only been invited to be the speaker. Behind the two of us stood many people praying for me. I understood that they were praying in an unknown tongue.

The dream was so surreal that I can remember today just how I was dressed for that awesome meeting. I wore a black suit, black shoes, black tie and held an oversized black Bible on the right side of my chest. The Bible stand, which I did not use, was rather tall to accommodate my height, but it was ever so crude in workmanship. Its appearance reminded me of the feed troughs we had used on the farm. I have no idea of its significance, but I do remember its appearance in such detail.

In my dream, I made three attempts to address the vast audience, and on each occasion, when I stepped forward with my Bible held high and tried to speak, the power of God fell so strongly that I was unable to speak a word. In my dream, I could see the Spirit. The Spirit looked like large waves of a silvery clouds coming down and rolling over, around, and throughout the entire sea of people. The picture that I saw reminded me of the visual observed on the Day of Pentecost: "And there appeared unto them cloven tongues like as of fire, and it sat upon each of them" (Acts 2:3, KJV).

My dream re-appeared in its entirety when I was twenty years old. Then, it reappeared again when I was twenty-two years old, but when I turned twenty-four years old, the dream did not appear as usual, and I heard a message only from someone from somewhere: "The dream will not appear again—just believe."

To this day, I have so many questions about the true meaning of the dream.

Even though I cannot tell the meaning of the dream that I had, the visual that I saw placed a burning desire within me to learn as much as I could about the Holy Spirit.

So, I began to develop the best bibliography on the subject of the Holy Spirit that I could possibly compile. Since that was in the early 1960s, I found resources most difficult to locate. My bibliography was very selective. I considered only those authors who had personally experienced the baptism of the Spirit and who had spoken in unknown tongues. I never considered the publications nor the essays written by others who said that the "gifts of the spirit" and physical healings had ceased with the New Testament apostles.

I visited on many occasions the site of the Schirra School House and the Holy Ghost outpouring in North Carolina that occurred in 1896. I read all that I could find about Charles Parham's revival in 1901 in Topeka, Kansas, Evan Roberts' revival in Wales in 1904, and William Seymore's revival on Azusa Street in California in 1903-1906.

I gathered all the available material that I could find that addressed A. J. Tomlinson's baptism in the Spirit in 1906.

With a passion, I followed the Holy Ghost revivals that swept across the college campuses during the 1970s period.

Then, one day, I was inspired to write a book called The Holy Ghost and Speaking in Tongues. It was published in several languages in 1983. I wanted to share my personal experience, but I especially wanted to encourage those who were seeking the Holy Spirit to follow the pattern of baptism and speak in tongues as revealed in the book of Acts, chapters 2, 8, 9, 10, and 19.

Finely, planting seed for my harvest reminded me of the old coffee can and the burlap bag that were so familiar in my day.

Both the coffee can and the burlap bag were symbols of two unwritten sharecropper's laws. The laws simply stated: "don't drink the prime water" and "don't eat the seed corn!" While it was neither a misdemeanor nor a felony to break either law, most folks upheld them religiously.

"Don't drink the prime water" referred to the old, rusty coffee can that was left filled with water at the water pump. The water in the can was used to prime the pump the next time cool water was needed. The process of priming was rather simple. One only had to pour the contents of the can of water into the top of the pump ever so gently, and then, with the other hand, one had to work the pump hand up and down with the same tenacity of fighting a grass fire on a March windy day.

At my first church, I looked for the can of prime water that I could use to start a spiritual outpouring, but sure enough, I found no prime water. As I recall, it certainly took a lot of emotional fasting and praying to get that old church pumping out fresh water again.

"Don't eat the seed corn" was the other sharecropper's law that I mentioned. That law referred to the sack of corn that each sharecropper put back at the end of the harvest. The sack of seed for specifically designated for the spring planting. I remember one cold and long winter that I found myself casting a wishful eye at Daddy's bag of yellow seed corn on several occasions. I could only imagine a fresh pan of Momma's hot cornbread, fresh-churned country butter, and thick molasses, but I knew better than to "eat the seed corn." It was seed for a new harvest.

Again, at my first church, I looked desperately for the sack of seed to plant for a needy harvest of souls, but the sack of seed could not be found. Either someone had eaten the seed corn, or the last pastor failed to leave me a sack of seed to plant.

However, it demanded more than a tin can and a burlap bag to get the spring planting done each year on our cotton farm. It required the cooperation of the whole family. Daddy made ready our small one-row planter. My older sister kept the grain flowing through the auger on that primitive planter. My brother and I followed along behind to make sure the grain fell on the ground in a mannerly fashion, and Momma kept an eye on the clock. At straight-up noon, she ordered us to table for the finest country cooking one could find.

When I began my pastoral ministry, I discovered real soon that I needed more than a can of water, a bag of corn, or a one row seed planter to impact the harvest at my church. I quickly realized that I needed the entire church to help me to prepare for the last days harvest. So, God inspired me to write and to publish a book entitled *Every Member a Worker, and A Special Work for Ever Member.*

My book was inspired my earlier life on Daddy's little cotton farm. The parables that Jesus taught about seed time and harvest provided theology and practicum, also.

Robert Louis Stevenson made a comment about planting seed that has always been a source of encouragement. There were too many years in my ministry that little sprang from my planting. Stevenson wrote, "Don't judge each day by the harvest you reap, but by the seeds that you plant."

In Mark 4:27ff (NKJV), Jesus provides great insight into the progression and the miracle of the planted seed. He says, "And the seed should sprout and grow, he himself does not know how."

In this passage, the master Teacher uses skillfully certain similes to explains the mysteries of the kingdom of God. His teachings are applicable to physical and spiritual growth of both plant and discipleship. I am told that the master Teacher is referring to the barley plant that grows readily in that region. However, I discovered that the indigenous barley plant resembles my native cotton plant. Both produce deep roots, stalks, stems, leaves, and fruit in a similar fashion.

As a boy, I was well aware of the growth and the maturity of the cotton plant. First came the beautiful velvety cotton leaves that were made possible by its deeply bedded root system. Each gorgeous leaf was complete with its own individual symmetry of embedded veins to form its structural design. When Daddy was not looking, I sometimes pulled some of the leaves to study the veins more intently. I would pretend that the veins in the leaves were roads to some adventurous wonderland in a far-off place. I imagined that I was making a journey to explore that land of mystery and enchantment.

However, Daddy was never pleased with just the pretty shiny leaves on the cotton plant. While he was grateful to know that the plant's roots were strong and healthy, he remained restless until the cotton bolls appeared on the stalk.

Jesus said that the barley plant would first produce a stalk, a limb, then form a leaf, and it was the same process of growth that the cotton plant achieved, but in the process of God's allotted time, the cotton leaves would make room for the cotton squares. The square was a green nodule that formed on the limb in a most mysterious fashion. The square was shaped in appearance like an itsy-bitsy soccer helmet, but the little fashionable nodule contained a nature-changing purpose. It would, in time, serve as the womb for the white hibiscus-like bloom that would soon burst from its self-containment.

How well I recall the days when I considered myself nothing but a "green pin-headed square." I was green in the Word, green in Pentecostalism, and green in preaching skills and styles. No one ever called me a narcist.

In a process of time, the green square on the cotton stalk gave birth to that long-awaited beautiful white bloom. The day after, the white bloom turned pink, and the day following, the pink bloom turned to a beautiful crimson red, but the day following the crimson red bloom, the bloom mysteriously fell to the ground, wilted, and died.

However, the red bloom would leave behind both its energy and paradigm. Mysteriously and unknown to man, the ugly little square was now charged with the dynamo to give birth to the magnificent cotton boll. The cotton boll would later produce eight to ten seeds for a bigger harvest. It was also endowed with thousands of silky strands of cotton suitable for the king's attire.

When I began my ministry as a teenager, there were many days the fruit of my ministry was not evident. I found myself saying many times, "God, if You have called me to preach Your Word, why do I have such small success?" God blessed others more than me, I thought. They always caught a "boatload of fish!" I seldom got a nibble. Some of my contemporaries reported more decisions of Christ in one evening of preaching than I could report for the entire summer revivals.

I shudder even today at the thoughts of those days when I labored with no noticeable success. I had nothing but leaves.

However, I recall so vividly the day my ministry produced its first white bloom. At last, my ugly perception of myself as a green square had finally changed. The phones rang off the hook. I was in great demand to speak, preach, teach, etc. Book offers escalated. Suddenly, mysteriously, and without my comprehension, my ministry was in great demand, but soon the white bloom of my ministry turned to red. Then, the red bloom turned loosed. Without fully comprehending the evolutional process, I stood silently and watched the red petal fall to the ground and die. My ministry had come full circle, and I knew now how!

Now, I cannot brag on my success. It was all the Lord's doing. Neither can I boast of my walk on God's directed path purposely designed for me.

Even if you were to ask my close friends to share their estimate of my effectiveness, their comments would certainly contain words substantiated only by faulty subjective opinions and their blinded love.

I like the way the Apostle Paul wraps up the product and the production of his ministry:

> For we are not bold to class or compare ourselves
> with some of those who commend themselves;
> but when they measure themselves by themselves
> and compare themselves with themselves, they
> are without understanding. But we will not boast
> beyond our measure, but within the measure of the
> sphere which God apportioned to us as a measure, to
> reach even as far as you.
>
> — 2 Corinthians 10:12-13 (NASB 1995)

> If you only look at us, you might well miss the
> brightness. We carry this precious Message around
> in the unadorned clay pots of our ordinary lives.
> That's to prevent anyone from confusing God's
> incomparable power with us. As it is, there's not
> much chance of that. You know for yourselves that
> we're not much to look at.
>
> — 2 Corinthians 4:7 (MSG)

Another version says it this way:

But we have this treasure in earthen vessels, so that
the surpassing greatness of the power will be of God
and not from ourselves;

— 2 Corinthians 4:7 (NASB 1995)

Protecting the Harvest

Protecting the harvest that God gave to me brings up some more old memories of the harvest years long ago.

Harvest time was an obvious time. It never required a clock, calendar, sermon, lecture, threat, or motivational lesson. Harvest time was the password of the household. It was the season that my whole family had lived and worked for during the entire year. We had fought the floods, the drought, the grass, and the weevils. We had taken our stand against the rats, mice, opossums, raccoons, deer, black birds, crows, and feral hogs. Now, we were prepared for our greatest work. We would stop at nothing to protect our harvest. Our harvest represented our hard work, or investment, and our future.

At harvest time was a personal time. I observed a spring in my Daddy's footstep that had gone missing during the long, hot summer days. I even caught the suspicious looks from the two hogs we planned to butcher come winter. Momma "put up" her usual jars of tomatoes, okra, bunch beans, pole beans, crowder peas, black eye peas, carrots, relish, cream corn, dill pickles, and cabbage, cauliflowers, and various tasty fruit preserves. My brother and I turned down the pages in the Sears-Roebuck catalog to mark our choices for new winter jeans, flannel shirts and two pairs of the long handle johns.

Even our old ring-eyed pooch, Arithmetic, barked incessantly to celebrate the occasion. We named him Arithmetic after he was run over by the mail truck. After that accident, he was never the same. He was permanently crippled. He had to put down three legs and carried the fourth just to be able to walk. 'Course, that's just an old dog story.

Harvest time was a sacrificial time. My brother and I were expected to miss the first three weeks of the fall school opening. Harvest time was more important than the opening of the school year. Daddy squeezed out every second of day light. Momma dragged a nine-foot cotton sack through the cotton field.

We all worked from sun-up to "dark-thirty." Our hogs ate by the moon light. Our chickens pecked corn in the dark.

Harvest time was a sacred time. Our whole household respected reverently the bountifulness of God's blessings on our hard work, and we all worshiped at the altar of hard work and sacrifice on each working day. The proper disposition and attitude were expected. No one approached harvest time in a half-hearted fashion. Discipline for the violation of these norms were known to be swift, painful, and certain.

In the book *Every Member A Worker* that I mentioned earlier, I shared three important lessons about harvest time which I gleaned on the farm. I learned that the harvest could not wait, that everyone was expected to participate, and that the harvest demanded the right attitude.

While I did not talk about "cotton" in that publication, I certainly drew from my "cotton-picking" theology just the same.

THEOLOGY OF SERVING

My theology of serving God was a long time in the making, and throughout the years I modified, edited, and altered it, but here is my theology of serving that I hold to today:

Jesus sets the example for serving:

> …That is what the Son of Man has done: He came

to serve, not be served—and then to give away his
life in exchange for many who are held hostage."

— Mark 10:45 (MSG)

Jesus died for my sins. That is more important to me than all the volumes of books that have been written about His purpose, prayers, promises, parables, miracles, teachings, and preaching.

I learned about what Jesus did for me when I was in elementary school. The teacher had placed a flannel board in front of my classroom. She cut out letters from John 3:16, which read, "For God so loved the world that He gave His only begotten Son, that whosoever believeth in him should not perish, but have everlasting life" (John 3:16, KJV), and placed the entire verse for all to read.

I often read it while I sat in class. I loved it. It made me feel wanted; and important. I believed it. But I didn't understand it. I really don't understand it today. How could God's only begotten Son love a poor sharecropper's son whose bare feet were hidden with embarrassment under his desk. I look forward to meeting Jesus someday.

Jesus makes the rules for serving:

...for without me ye can do nothing.

— John 15.5 (KJV)

Jesus guarantees our success:

I can do all things through Him who strengthens me.

— Philippians 4:13 (NASB 1995)

Paul provides the right attitude for serving:

Even if I am executed here and now, I'll rejoice to

being an element in the offering of your faith that
you make on Christ's altar…

— Philippians 2:17 (MSG)

At this juncture of my life, I do not regret that I chose to serve the Lord. After all, if I had not chosen to serve Christ, I would have served Satan, self, or sin. However, because of Jesus, who chose me first, I made the right choice, and the right choice made me!

HAND OF GOD

When I attended the McClelland Church of God in the late 1940s, I heard a young girl sing these few lines to a song: "Jesus use me, please Lord don't refuse me, for surely there's a work for me to do, and even though it's humble, Lord, help my will to crumble, and though the price be great I'll work for you." After I heard those words for the first time, I sang it hundreds of times later as I worked the cotton fields, strolled the banks of Bear Slough, and walked along the railroad tracks to pray.

Jesus called me to serve Him. I failed Him so many times. I stumbled countless of times. I complained most of the time, and I grumbled all the time, but He never fired me. He just reached down with His hand of mercy, picked me up, and put me right back into His work.

The hand of God touched my eyes one day. I had once gazed upon the evangelist who was drenched in perspiration when he placed his hands on me, prayed, and I was divinely healed.

However, when Jesus touched my eyes, I looked at the long lines of youth who "prayed through" at old dusty altars in the youth camp revivals where I was asked to preach. Later, I witnessed hundreds of young college students as they walked walk upfront of others to make decisions for Christ. I saw the old, one-eyed "wine-o," whom I had known as a kid, pray the sinner's prayer, then close his one eye and die. I saw the mother of four little children take her last breath. Then, she made her flight in to glory of heaven. I saw the man who had been congested with bitterness for twenty years make a surprise appearance one Sunday morning. I saw him repent with tears. Then, I saw the hill above the church where the log truck came speeding down and struck and killed him the following Sunday. I saw many couples hold hands, pray, and forgive one another just in time to save their marriages, children, and homes, and I saw bitterness, envy, jealous, strife, hatred, and malice fade away and die at the foot of the cross of Jesus.

The Bible says, "Then the eyes of the blind shall be opened, And the ears of the deaf shall be unstopped" (Isaiah 35:5, NJKV).

Then, the hand of the Lord touched my ears. As a boy, I could tell the sound of a lark, mockingbird, sparrow, cardinal or a crow. I knew the voice of a nightingale. I recognized the cooing of the morning dove, and I heard the sound of thunder and the roar of the flood as it washed our spring crop away in a mighty torrent.

After Jesus touched my ears, I heard voices as though they were many waters that came from the thousands of Chinese Christians who prayed hours each night in the basement of an old, cold church for a revival in mainland China. I heard the hellish voices of demons. The evil spirits cried out in anger at the name of Jesus Christ, and I heard the old man plead in a dying whisper: "Son, promise me now that you will meet me over yonder, on that bright and peaceful shore!"

And the eyes of them that see shall not be dim, and
the ears of them that hear shall hearken.

— Isaiah 32:3 (KJV)

Jesus also touched the lips of mine. I had once preached to the trees that grew at the end of the cotton rows. I spoke often to the little creatures who scampered along the old railroad track where I walked and prayed. I shouted my make-believe sermons at the giant cypress trees that grew in the middle of Bear Slough.

However, the day that Jesus touched these sun-parched lips of clay, I told everyone who listened how I received the Holy Spirit and spoke in tongues. Then, I preached a revival in my home church. I spoke at a hidden gravesite tucked deeply in the darkness of the hard wood timber. Only a teenage couple who held their still born baby placed in a cardboard box, the undertaker, and I were at the shadowy burial place.

I shared the gospel of Good News in pulpits from the Atlantic to the Pacific. I proclaimed the Master's saving grace to others in brush arbors, musky tents, storefront churches, court house lawns, cruise boats, beaches, college dorms, block buildings, brick building, board and batten buildings, rest homes, prison houses, half-way houses, radio stations, and open pavilions. I just preached wherever I could brag on Jesus. My world was small; my message was big.

> Go therefore and make disciples of all the nation,
> baptizing them in the name of the Father and the
> Son and the Holy Spirit, teaching them to observe
> all that I commanded you; and lo, I am with you
> always even to the end of the age.
>
> — Matthew 28:19-20 (NAV)

God's hand took my hand, and the two of us walked together. With two small, dirty hands of a little farm boy, I once crafted a small guitar fashioned from a lard can lid, a willow branch, and old rusty bailing wire. I made the musical instrument so that I could sit in the window at the country church and make music with the big boys during the summer revival.

However, after God touched my hands, I held the noses of hundreds of believers who were baptized in cattle troughs, swimming pools, bar ditches, ponds, rivers, the Jordan River, hospital beds, and their death beds.

These hands held tiny babies poised for dedication while their grandparents cried and the little tykes held my fingers.

These hands have held numerous wedding rings, hundreds of obituaries, and thousands of communion cups.

These hands have anointed with olive oil the heads of drunks, demon-possessed, druggies, derelicts, deceived, helpless, hopeless, paralyzed, paranoid, confused, contrary, incontinent, incarcerated, terminally ill, and incurably diseased people—all in the powerful name of Jesus Christ.

> In your name I will lift up my hands.
>
> — Psalms 63:4 (MT).

(Just for the curious minds who wanted to know if the little hand-crafted guitar functioned well—heavens, no, but no one noticed! We were having revival!)

Finally, God's hands even touched these two feet of mine. Only God knew just how adventurous these two feet of mine had been. As a barefooted private investigator, I must have discovered every mud hole, bar ditch, saw brier, sticker grass, cut-grass, cockle bur, jagged stone, broken fruit jar, rusty nail, barbed wire, slimy slug, copper head, thorn bush, and fire ant mound that existed in those secret places on Daddy's little twenty-acre cotton farm.

One day, these two feet of mine retraced the steps of Jesus from Gethsemane to the Easter Gate, from Mt. Calvary to the empty tomb, and from Bethany to Mt. Ascension.

> He brought me up also out of an horrible pit, out of the miry clay, and set my feet upon a rock, and established my goings.
>
> — Psalms 40:2 (KJV)

R. Lloyd Black

Henry Wadsworth Longfellow talks about footprints in his poem, "A Psalm of Life!"

> "Lives of... men will remind us
> We can make our lives sublime
> And departing leave behind us
> Foot prints on the sands of time.
> Footprints that perhaps another
> Sailing over life's solemn main
> A forlorn and shipwrecked brother
> Seeing shall take heart again.
> Let us then be up and doing
> With a heart for any fate
> Still achieving, still pursuing
> Learn to labor and to wait."

Paul said, "...How beautiful are the feet of those who bring good news of good things" (Romans 10:15, NASB 1995).

SUMMARY AND APPLICATION

Just for the record, I struggled on my pathway of serving, but in my struggle, God's love transitioned me, and God's mercy repositioned me.

By His Spirit, God removed me from the peaceful environment of the sharecropper's son. Then, by His grace, He baptized this obscure servant into the hostile society of humanistic thinking and global hatred.

Then, God said, "Preach only the gospel of the Good News to this complex ethnic culture of enmity and suspicion. My grace will do the rest."

- Can you describe and illustrate your own personal call to serve the Lord Jesus Christ? What biblical references can you cite to substantiate that invitation? Describe your affirmation. What confirmation did your local church provide?

- In the Old Testament, you may consider the example of God's call to Samuel. See in 2 Samuel chapters 2 and 3. In the New Testament, you may consider the call of Saul who was later called Paul. See Acts 9.

- How would you explain Jesus' comment written in John 15:5b?

- Have you experienced a "miracle" in your life? What did you learn from it? How can that miracle apply to the winning of someone to Jesus Christ? You may reread the miracle in the life of the Gadarene in Mark 5.

THE PATHS OF
Sifting

In all your ways acknowledge Him, and He shall
direct your paths.

— Proverbs 3:6 (NKJV)

PREDECESSORS SIFTING

In "The Paths of Sifting," both my predecessor and I will share insights about certain past events in our lives. When my great grandfather related his story, I felt as though I were standing alongside him. His emotional account of his relationship with General George Washington enabled me to sense his fears and tears.

Amasa Mitchell was my third great grandfather. He was not a pastor as many of my other relatives were, but he was a servant of the people just the same. Amasa devoted his entire youth to help build the foundations of American freedom. In an interview given to his grandson, Dr. Francis Asbury Mitchell, M.D., Amasa sifted through several war epics of his illustrious life. Because of the historical significance of his war stories, I wanted to share one account with you. Amasa's interview follows:

> "In just a few days, I will turn 90, I think, 'cause I
> was born in 1761. Mom and Papa had just arrived
> from Ireland—they barely got me here!" Dr. Mitchell
> watched patiently as Amasa tearfully squeezed out
> his emotional thoughts through those thin and
> wrinkled lips.

"Perhaps my greatest memory of my youth is the day that I told the recruiter I was eighteen. I wanted to be in the colonial militia—I wanted to be a soldier, but truthfully, I was really scared of the war that was about to happen. As I remember, the recruiter measured all six feet of me but said that I was too skinny and frail to tote a gun and a belongings sack at the same time. So, he took my name. Then, he handed me a fife. At that, I was much disappointed, but he explained to me that I could lead the soldiers with the fife and with the help of the little drummer boy. That pleased me well. After all, some told me I was pretty good with that musical thing, and while I never considered myself as being good in music, I already knew how to play the march tunes really good. It was not what I wanted, but I stood tall, smiled, and saluted the recruiter. I signed my "X," picked up my fife, and I listened the boys as they whistled and called me "fifer boy!"

"My decision to join George Washington's army was based on my love for this country and my admiration for General George. General George was tall, kind, could make decisions, and he prayed a lot. He seemed to size me up really good when he was told that I was the fifer.

They told me before I signed my "X" that there were no army uniforms, shoes, or guarantee of meals. 'Course, we already knew there was no money. Some of the boys were upset because there was no whiskey or tobacco. I was a Christian and belonged to the Methodist Church back home, so I never touched the stuff. I never was tempted to touch the devil's stuff.

"I watched General Washington many times as he slipped into the woods before the battles. I often followed and heard his prayers. He almost always wanted to find a fallen tree to use for an altar. Then he prayed. I never let him know that I took my hat off all the time he prayed. I knew that was the reason we won the war. General George had God working for us.

"I remember one march around Brandywine. It was the hardest. We went three days with no food. The enemy tracked us by seeing the blood from our feet that was mixed with the sleet and snow. None of us had shoes. One out of every six of us died on the march and in the battle.

"I remember the cold Christmas night and the large junks of ice ... four and five feet thick over the Delaware River. No one would expect us to cross that river in such bitter cold, but General George said, "Go," and we went. I found out later that it was a daring thing to do, but I knew General George would get us through, and he did.

"I remember when Benedict Arnold was caught for treason. It was hard for me to believe that he would do such a thing. We really cared for Benedict. Too bad! No one expected that, for sure, and I played the fife for the executional march to the hanging tree where his accomplice, John Andre, was hanged. It was a sad day. I cried. All of us cried, including General Washington. Andre was so educated, a painter, and master of so many things; he was only thirty-two.

"The winter of Valley Forge was so hard on us and the wives who had come up and the little children. Most of the animals died. It was difficult to bear the stench of the dead carcasses of horses. A few hundred men were encamped. Most of us were just teenagers. We had little to no food, slept on dirt floors, and wrapped cold bloody feet in soft straw, but we were proud soldiers. Sometimes I played the fife to cheer the spirits. Sometimes I was just too hungry to play. We went one time three days with no food.

"But my greatest memory was when 'we won' and the British Army was tired of our hardness and refusal to give up. The American army was drawn up and witnessed the stacking of the British Arms. Then, old Cornwallis delivered up his sword; when I saw his sword laid down, I knew the war was over."

"And what was your overall feeling after two years of freezing, hungering, working without pay, and seeing your friends run through with a bayonet?" Dr. Mitchell asked Amasa.

With eyes flooded with tears and a heart filled with pain, Dr. Mitchell heard his grandfather say, "I looked over the landscape on that beautiful day and fought back tears because we had fought so bitterly for so long, and I said, 'My country! My home! I thank God for permitting me to be here this day and see the dawn of American liberty!'"

Then, his grandfather smiled. He reached out with a shaking hand, touched his grandson's shoulder, and said, "I would gladly do it again!"

Signed: Francis Asbury Mitchell, M.D.[1]

As a postscript to Amasa's story, allow me to share my latest discovery.

I recently discovered that a marker was erected on the Valley Forge battlefield. The marker tells the story of the dreadfully cold winter that characterizes the battle at that scene, but the marker also contains plaque, and on that plaque are the names of hundreds of teenage boys who fought and died at that battle to ensure our freedom.

One of the names that is inscribed on that is Amasa Mitchell— one of my great grandfathers.

The smile that Amasa gave to his grandson at the conclusion of that interview reminds me of a quote by Dr. Seuss: "Don't cry because it's over, smile because it happened."

ASSOCIATION WITH SIFTING

Like Amasa Mitchell, I can smile today. My life has been both eventful and blessed, but my life has also been filled with a long list of challenges. J. Marine is accredited to having said, "Challengers are what makes life interesting, and overcoming them is what makes life meaningful."

My life has been blessed with challenges, but my life has also been very meaningful.

So, when I decided to sift through my life and to review some of the challenges that I had overcome, I hardly knew where to begin, but I reached that point in my life that I was determined to "sift through the past and to see what I could uncover."

The sifting process actually began at the ending of the year. My church, my church associates, and myself were working methodically to complete the year-end requirements, programs, reports, etc. and to dive enthusiastically into the Christmas holidays.

Then, the phone rang, and I was reminded to be at the Pastoral Appreciation Banquet the following night at 7 P.M. I really have a lot to do, I thought, But I must honor the generous invitation from my Gideon friends. I am so glad that I did, because not only was the food excellent, but I got a handle on how to "sift through the annals of my life's past."

That evening at the Gideons banquet, I heard a powerful message from God's powerful Word. The guest speaker reminded us to view life "through the windshield and not through the rearview mirror!" He aptly drew well-crafted and pointed comparisons and contrasts about the two different views of life, and after that powerful sermon, I was determined to view my personal life "more widely and clearly."

However, wouldn't you know? As soon as I sat down in my old antique Ford truck to begin the journey back home, I methodically reached to adjust my rearview mirror. My aim was to back off the dimly lighted parking lot as safely as possible, and with the aid of my rearview mirror, I was able to dodge one of the old preachers who attended the event, two garbage cans, one mop dropped on the curb, two mongrel dogs that had obliterated the third garbage can and a mud puddle filled with greasy ice particles.

Then, I made my way from the banquet hall to the big bridge that crossed the Arkansas River. I was headed to the house when suddenly, I was amazed at the beauty of the sight that lay before me. The stars that had been hidden during the early period of cold winter rain had now burst forth from their coverings in the clearing skies. The stary lights reminded me of little energetic children church dancers at the Christmas pageant.

Looking through my windshield, I could see thousands of varied Christmas lights that marked the architect and shape of houses, trees, and lawns. It appeared to me that everyone in my town had attempted to tell the story of the babe born in Bethlehem. The sight was stupendous! It was easy to see that it was Christmastime in the city, and there I sat in my old truck, looking through the windshield at God's great hour.

Wouldn't you know it! I was reminded immediately with the blinking lights and honking of the horn that I was going too slowly and occupying both lanes. Without thinking, I glanced at my rearview

R. Lloyd Black

mirror. I wanted to cast an angry eye of disdain at the disrespectable and immature driver behind me!

Now that I have reach a special milestone in my life, I wanted to look through the rearview mirror of my life. I wanted to see just what all that I had left behind me.

However, when I looked back through the rearview mirror of my life, I was amazed at the two-sided persona of time. In one way, time reminded me of a flying squirrel being chased by a hungry owl. By that I mean time passed so swiftly.

In another way, time reminded me of the frustrated land turtle who attempted to negotiate the land mines left on Omaha Beach.

Like that old turtle, I had to walk slowly and very cautiously on my pathway through life to avoid the numerous land mines that had been hidden purposely to destroy me and my family.

When look back to see what was behind, I was reminded of the groves of dense fishing cane that grew along the edges Bear Slough. The cane had served my brother and me well with our need for fishing poles.

We two loving brothers had often used the green and limber canes to fasten green cotton bolls at the cane's end. The green and limber cane stick worked excellently to launch a hard, green cotton boll at the other's hind side.

The cane sticks had a docile purpose, too. The canes could be also used to place as markers in the cotton field to mark the progress of our work.

On some occasions, my brother and I drove a stake into the cotton middle, far ahead of the point where we started our day's work. We wanted to see just how close to the stake we could get before the close of day.

On other days, we would drive a stake down at the point where we began our new day's work. We wanted to see just how far ahead of the stick we could pick cotton before we grew too tired to pick another boll.

Either way, the stakes served as motivational objects for our day. They marked special places of importance in our long day of chopping or picking cotton.

So, when I decided to sift through my past, I wanted to mark a few areas of my life that served as motivational catalysts in my work for the Lord.

For one, I wanted to place a stake in several places to mark both the places and faces of significance while on my life's journey. I also wanted to learn if I had remained faithful to my single purpose in life. Finally, I wanted to see what changes in life I had made on my walk with God.

Places of Significance

THE PLACE CALLED "GRACE"

The most significant place in my life is a place called "grace." Here, I drove down my first stake to mark a significant place in my life. The place called "grace" was an important place because it was there that God saved me by grace through faith.

Paul says it this way: "For by grace, you have been saved through faith, and that not of yourselves; it is the gift of God" (Ephesians 2:8, NKJV).

However, frankly, I cannot remember the actual time nor the actual place where the Lord saved me by His amazing grace, but I can remember the "Bawl Bearing Quartet!" The Bawl Bearing Quartet often visited the little country church where I attended. The spokesperson for the quartet said that his group would do the bawling if we would just do the bearing. Frankly, I liked the quartet singing quite well. They usually sang one of my favorite songs. It talked about a time and place. It went something like this: "I remember the time / I can take you to the place / where the Lord saved me / by His saving grace."

Even though the words did not completely resonate with me, I always enjoyed singing right along with them.

The place called "grace" did not have a miraculous setting like the Ethiopian had on the desert when Evangelist Philip appeared out of thin air to minister to him. Neither did it come with all the excitement that Cornelius enjoyed when Peter preached to him and his household. It never had the mystique nor the theology that surrounded Nicodemus when he asked Jesus how to be born-again, and neither did it come with the light and sound effects that Paul experienced on the road to Damascus.

However, I was saved by grace just the same.

Frankly, I used to consider my Christian testimony to be just plain country-bland. I didn't have a testimony of deliverance from alcohol, drugs, or demon oppression. I had never been in a jail. I was never on death row. I didn't get saved in a WWII fox hole.

While I may not be able to recall all of the pertinent data of my salvation experience, I do remember the hundreds of times that I went to the altar to ask God to forgive me. Every fall, I had to repent for going to the ten-cent picture show. I loved to watch Johnny Mack Brown, Tim Holt, Gene, Roy, Lash LaRue, Wild Bill Hickock, Durango Kid, Cisco Kid, Billy the Kid, Kit Carson, Tim Maynard, Hoot Gibson, Tom Mix, Tex Ritter, and most of all, my favorite, The Lone Ranger. I can still see that silver screen in that old Cotton Plant theater.

Wouldn't you know, I was always condemned for reading comic books. I had my stack of comics, for sure. Once or twice a year, I would meet my friend Elmo and we would spend a whole hot summer afternoon haggling and trading funny books, but when the next church service rolled around, I had to go to the altar and repent for reading such stuff.

My greatest sin burden hung over me like a dark cloud. It was guilt. Guilt surfaced every time that my brother and me smoked "possum grapevines." Oh, if my Momma had only known! After I smoked my fill and my tongue and mouth were so sore from the sap from the partially dried grapevine, I would live in fear and tremble. "Oh God, don't send me to that fiery hell that the preacher done told us about," I would pray.

However, somewhere back in those dusty altars at the Church of God in McClelland, Arkansas, I made it all right with God. I was saved by grace. I had no money and nothing to trade, but God did not want anything that I had. He just wanted me. So, I believed that Jesus died for my sins, arose on the third day, and lives for evermore. I still believe it, just like that. My theology hasn't moved past that truth yet. I still don't understand all there is to know about grace, but I sure like what Paul told me about grace:

> Saving is all his idea, and all his work. All we do
> is trust him enough to let him do it. It's God's gift
> from start to finish! We don't play the major role. If
> we did, we'd probably go around bragging that we'd
> done the whole thing! No, we neither make nor save
> ourselves. God does both the making and saving.
> He creates each of us by Christ Jesus to join him in
> the work he does, the good work that he has gotten
> ready for us to do, work we had better be doing.
>
> — Ephesians 2:8-10 (MSG)

At the place called "grace," I stood while Jesus placed one arm around me and took the other and wrote my name in the Lamb's book of life, and for all the above reasons, I sing quite often the phrase that Johnny Cash made popular: "I was there when it happened, and I guess I oughta know!"

The second place where I want to put down a stake is the place called "sagacity." The word sagacity is just another name for "discretion." It actually means "the cautious use of words which could divulge information that should be kept private."

I am glad that I put down a stake at the place called "sagacity." This is the place where I learned that much of my relationship with Christ is personal and must ever be classified information.

I learned about the place called "sagacity" in the 1960s. I was commissioned by the state overseer of the churches to write his biography. I was honored, challenged but receptive. After all, he was an internationally known clergyman. He had achieved worldwide renown, and most of us young preachers attempted to imitate his style and mannerisms. We longed for his charisma, wide appeal, and wisdom.

Now, I am so thankful that I accepted his invitation to write his life's story. He taught me so much about sagacity. His first lesson about sagacity began with his request for the title of his book. He wanted the book to be named *Yet Not I*. His title tips the tale of his theology. The overseer insisted his biography to be about Christ's ministry in him. He flatly refused to allow me to write about his ministry in Christ. I caught on right away just what he meant by that. During the development and the publication of his biography, he took a stern position with me. He made certain that I did not expose his personal roots in Christ for the pleasure of others to review. "Brother Lloyd," he would say, "My life with Christ is hidden. You be sure that no one sees me, but Christ that lives within me. I died the day I left the coal mine in Kentucky, and the life that I now live is in Christ; I live, yet not I, but the Christ that is in me lives!"

He seldom shared that revelation about himself with me that he did end the familiar phrase by "speaking in tongues" and dancing a jig or two!

During that period of writing his story, I put down a stake at a place called "sagacity." From that day forward, I determined not to expose my roots for the judgment of others.

Jesus talks about "roots" in one of His parables:

> "Listen. What do you make of this? A farmer planted
> seed. As he scattered the seed, some of it fell on
> the road and birds ate it. Some fell in the gravel it
> sprouted quickly but didn't put down roots, so when
> the sun came up it withered just as quickly.
>
> — Mark 4:3-6 (MSG)

From His parable, we not only learn that "roots" beget life and sustain growth, but we also learn that God designed roots to function out of sight and out of light. Once roots are exposed to light, they soon die as revealed in Christ's comments.

Can you remember the malady of Hezekiah? He became exalted with wealth that he had inherited. He ignorantly revealed his hidden wealth to the eyes of his enemy. Then, his enemy came back and seized Hezekiah's wealth (Isaiah 39).

I was first enlightened on this subject through the writings of Watchman Nee. Pastor Nee was the minister of the Hong Kong church. His published work in *Twelve Baskets Full 2* in the 1960s contained the following quote: "By His grace, God has accomplished something through us, but do remember that what He has accomplished is not matter for advertisement or propaganda. If we expose the work of God, we shall find that the touch of death will come upon it immediately; and the loss will correspond to the extent to which we uncover results."

In this short semi-autobiography of myself, I determined to keep a truckload of my personal life covered. My life has certainly been blessed. My ministry has reaped a harvest of rare miracles, answered prayers, prophetic insights, utterances, and spiritual blessings, but the roots of those divine blessings run the danger of death if exposed to others. God's grace saved me, then God's gifts defined me. What I am, who I am, and where I go from here is in God's hands.

I no longer pace to and fro seeking franticly a Rema word of knowledge, a word of wisdom, a prophetical utterance, a dream, a vision, or a mystical phrase just to keep my name and my voice in public. I want to keep the source of my life and the power that sustains me hidden in my roots of faith lest they be exposed and die.

THE PLACE CALLED "PERCEPTION"

The third place that I will drive down a stake is a place called "perception." The place called "perception" is where I finally accepted the fact of who I am in the Lord.

"Perception" is defined as "a process by which one regards, analyses, retrieves, and reacts to any kind of information from his environment and makes moral decisions based on the process."

Business Jargons provides for its clients a framework to comprehend the function of perception. It explains the concept of perception in five distinctive steps: object, awareness, recognition, interpretation, and response.

This series of steps depicted accurately my personal journey of perception. While I was graciously aware of the love and happiness experienced in my early childhood, I was equally aware of the socioeconomical gap between me and my peers. That gap stymied my self-image and dwarfed my self-esteem. I submitted outwardly to my family "barely making ends meet," but I cowered inwardly with fear, doubt, pessimism and depression because of that lack. Unknowingly, my perception of myself was mirrored by others. My "in-look" determined my "outcome!"

Then, one day I read the story of Gideon in the book of Judges 6:11. I found with delight a resemblance of his story with mine. Gideon was the son of a poor farmer. So, I saw right off that I could identify with that setting (see verse 15).

The story of Gideon tells us that an "angel of the Lord" visited Gideon. The angel gave him a promise of good news and blessings, but because Gideon had lived for so long in fear and disbelief, he refused the promise and chose instead to live on explanation.

However, God eventually poured His Spirit out on Gideon. Then, God called others to follow him. It was all God's doing, but even with the Spirit, Gideon vacillated. It took a while for the Spirit to lead and to empower Gideon to be the leader God intended.

I went through a long period of fear and doubting, even after God poured His Spirit out on me and called others to follow me. I struggled to believe that God chose me, with little talent, knowledge, and people skills. If God had only asked me, I could have enlightened Him on others who were more talented and capable than I.

Today, I live on promises and not explanations. I left all of my inferiority complexes at the place called "perception." My "in-look" was changed to make room for my outcome.

I learned to define myself the way that God sees me. Christ said:

> You didn't choose me, remember; I chose you, and put you in the world to bear fruit, fruit that won't spoil. As fruit bearers, whatever you ask the Father in relation to me, he gives you.
>
> — John 15:16 (MSG)

Next, I allowed Paul to express my new feelings about myself:

> I identified myself completely with him. Indeed, I have been crucified with Christ. My ego is no longer central. It is no longer important that I appear righteous before you are have your good opinion, and I am no longer driven to impress God. Christ lives in me. The life you see me living is not "mine," but it is lived by faith in the Son of God, who loved

me and gave himself for me. I am not going to go
back on that.

— Galatians 2:20 (MSG)

THE PLACE CALLED "REMINISCENCE"

The fourth place that I will mark is the place called "reminiscence."

The place called "reminiscence" brings to mind a fitting quote by S. Gale: "Never forget where you are going. Never lose sight of where you are going. Never take for granted the people who traveled with you."

On God's directed path, I met thousands of people and hundreds of others who impacted my life. I'm sorry to say I took too many of them for granted, but I never forgot their contributions to my life and to my ministry.

At the place called "reminiscence," I see vividly a wall of portraits that were painted with the soft touch of sweet memories. Each painted portrait is a face of a person who walked with me in this life.

Some of those faces that I see are the images of my own family. My Mother, Daddy, twin brother, and sisters only walked a while with me, but our time spent together on life's highway was encouraging, comforting, and loving. Most of them now walk with Christ on His golden streets save one sister and my twin. We still talk. My twin and I call each other at least three times a day. Thank God for cell phones.

Some are the faces on that wall of painted portraits are individuals who poured themselves into making me whom I am today. There is the face of my elementary school teacher, my pastor when I was a teenager, my junior high school English teacher, my professor at the school of theology, and the faces of those whom God sent to follow me as I followed the Lord.

I can still trace the lines of fellowship in the faces of Lester M., Jimmy F., Walter H., Bobby M., Dennis P, Raymond S, Chester S., Orval D., Floyd H., Compy G., Doewer C., T.J.L., George W., John W., Robert M, Ralph E., Ray S., Shawn O., Clarence and Helen R.,

Jean H, and many of their families. They kept the doors opened for me. They left the light on! They prayed for my encouragement. They respected to my wife and my children. It was Aitchison who said, "Trust your journey. Trust the process. Raise your energy and the right people will come into our life." God certainly sent just the right people into my life.

Many of the faces that I see on the wall of reminiscence are the faces of my "marathon friends." My marathon friends all processed common characteristics. They knew me well, but they still loved me. They witnessed the few achievements that accomplished in life, but they refused to be critical or jealous. They were members at my church at some point and time, but they never ceased to call me "pastor!"

Some were the faces of my "fourth generation friends." My fourth generation friends showered my wife and me at our wedding, provided needed funds for the welfare of our children, and continued their gifts of finances, prayers, and love for our grands, but they never stopped. They continue to pour out gifts of love and affection upon our great grandchildren. They just won't stop. They have walked with me through four generations. Now, they give to me both the spark and the determination to continue my journey for the rest of the way.

On the wall of portraits at the place called "reminiscence" are faces of two angels who stand out above all the others. They are the faces of my dear children. I painted their faces with love and tears. I see their faces right now as though they were at the moment of their birth. Each face was well-defined by both tranquility and peace while they snuggled at their mother's breast. I saw them again, today. I observed with compassion the looks on both of their faces. Each bore the lines and marks of anxiety and love. The compassionate strokes of anxiety and love are reserved by the artist to paint the faces of parents who dearly love their children.

There is still one portrait that is the sweetest face of all. It is placed in the center of the wall at the place called "reminiscence." It is the face of the person that I see each morning when I first awake. It is the face of the lady of my heart, my house, and my happiness. It is the face behind my accomplishments, successes, and achievements. It is the face of my silent companion who walked with me each step of my way. It is the face of my wife. She never left me, and I wonder, "Why?" She never criticized me, but she had so many reasons, and she never complained even though I relegated her and my children to second place behind the demands of the church.

She is, as an unknown author said, the "only star in my walk of fame!"

My walk with God has been long and somewhat grievous at times, but it has also been rewarding and fulfilling, and when I look back, I confess that I feel a twitch in my heart sense a tear in my eye. There are places and faces that I may never see again, but I'm not crying because so much has ended. I'm smiling because it happened.

Assessment of Purpose

I really like a quote that I read by S. Maraboli: "To embark on the journey toward your goals and dreams require bravery—to remain on that path requires courage. Commitment is the merger of the two."

So, I looked through my rearview mirror just to assess my commitment to the purpose of my life. It was never difficult for me to know my purpose. I could rattle it off quickly with only six simple words: "To serve God and His church." However, I could state it much easier than I could live it.

Looking back, I can see numerous opportunities that afforded me an exit from my purpose. I always wanted to exit when my pathway got bumpy. Each exit I saw when my pathway became bumpy led to beautiful green pastors. The grass sure looked greener and most inviting!

Had it not been for the grace of God, I would have exited a number of times. There were excellent financial offers, military chaplaincy offers, hospital chaplaincy offers, business partnership offers, situations, circumstances, pressures, spiritual droughts, rebukes, misunderstandings, envies, strives, bickering, backbiting, bellyaching, bitterness, lies—I'm sure you get the drift. However, in all this, God passionately held onto me. Consequently, because of His grip on me, I was able to walk out and to freshen out my purpose in life.

Did I ever want to quit? Yes! I once quit three times on the way to preach the Sunday morning sermon. I recall on one particular Lord's day, I rehearsed a mean speech. I intended to give the whole congregation a dose of real "truth!" I had adamantly ignored the love sermon that Jesus had spoken to me to share that day, and as soon as I walked into the door, an erring brother threw his arms around me, sobbed bitterly, and thanked me for "being patient and loving." Wow! Both God and I knew that I was the one standing in the need of patience and love.

On another occasion, I asked the Lord "Why should I stay and put up with this mess?" Then, the Spirit spoke softly to my angry heart, "Because you love these people," and I said, "Lord, you're looking at the wrong information sheet. My love for this bunch has done left out!"

Then, God poured a bucket of grace right out in my heart. My eyes flooded with tears. "You're correct, God, I do love this church," I said, but that was not the last time that I wanted to quit. Oh, no! I was guilty of wanting to quite every Monday on that deep, dark, day of depression. I could sing old Gorge Jones line for line and verse for verse: "Lord, I must have left her a thousand times, but I'm not ready it!"

While my purpose never changed, my goals changed. Some of my goals were reached, adjusted, altered, and even abandoned. Each season of my life demanded setting new goals and adjusting or abandoning the old. For the most part, my goals became shorter in range, and I made sure that my goals were manageable. I kept reminding myself, "You're not the age you were when you started!"

My goals changed; my life changed, but my purpose never changed.

As I look back at the landmarks behind me, I am reminded of statement made by the great Charles Dickens: "The best way to lengthen out our days is to walk steadily and with a purpose!"

Many years ago, I claimed the following Bible references in my attempt to maintain my purpose:

> The Lord will fulfill His purpose for me; your
> steadfast love, O Lord, endures forever. Do not
> forsake the work of your hands.
>
> — Psalms 138:8 (ESV)

> I cry out to God Most High, to God who will fulfill
> his purpose for me. He will send help from heaven
> to rescue me...
>
> — Psalms 57:2-3 (NLT)

Winston Churchill once said, "It's not enough to have lived; we should be determined to have lived for something."

I attempted to live with purpose, and my purpose was to serve God and His church.

I wish I were able to give someone the credit for the following poem. I personally think that it is a very good poem. I read it often. I can see myself in the poem. My experience, resolve, and hope are expressed in the beautiful poetry:

> "As I climb up its hill
> Slopes and jagged edges and all
> There are times I slip but still
> At no time did I fall
>
> As I tread along its way
> Sometimes I run into bends

Stumbling blocks on some days
But never into dead ends

As I sprint down its lanes
Huddles seem to abound
Yet the tripping now and again
Still can't bring me down

Whims of life that lie in wait
Though I may not have a clue
Firm is my will, strong is my faith
My God will see me through."

—Unknown

The Changes I Made in Life

Many changes that I made in life came to my mind as I looked through the rearview mirror of my life.

Enthusiastically, I began to scribble down the changes as they presented themselves. My, according to what I was remembering, I had made a lot of changes. I pinched myself to see if I was the same person that I thought I was.

Pat helped me to redefine my changes. Some, she said, were never realized. Others, she suggested, needed to be fine-honed. Then, she informed me, "You have to be kidding. This has not been changed!"

So, I tore up the first draft of changes made in my life and sat at hand to draft the second.

For the most part, Pat sort of agreed with my second draft. I'm not sure she is fully on board with this list, but here it is. Here are the top ten changes that I made in my life while on God's directed pathway:

- Number Ten: I decided that someone might want to read my story after all.

- Number Nine: I now spend more time with optimistic friends and try to avoid pessimistic people as much as possible.

- Number Eight: I still accept responsibility because I am the pastor, but refuse to accept the blame when it is not my fault.

- Number Seven: I feed my faith on the Word of God and starve my fears.

- Number Six: I learned to say, "No," and "I don't know," much more easily. I don't know the answer anymore, but I am aware of the problem.

- Number Five: I relax more, but I'm still working on this one. I still pastor a church!

- Number Four: I eat less, make healthier choices, and avoid meats, breads, sweets, sugar, and salt! I'm still trying to make myself drink more water!

- Number Three: I "attempt" to pray more and to do less busy church work.

- Number Two: I give my wife and my children preference over the demands of the church. This one had a little difficulty making the canon. By that I mean that Pat was not fully in agreement.

- Number One: I desire to know Jesus, and not just about Jesus. I now seek His heart, and not just His hand.

Now that I have looked back through the rearview mirror at my life, I am grateful that I visited one more time the places and faces of significance. I have been encouraged to know that I have maintained purpose of life even though at times I had a tuff time keeping the faith. Equally important, my walk on God' pathway sustained me but also changed me.

So, you may want to ask: am I the person whom I wanted to be at the end of my journey?

The answer to that question is both a "no" and a "yes!"

"No." I have to admit there were images of over-realized grandeur of myself that I had personally fabricated. Even though I struggled with both a low self-esteem and self-image, I was also capable of vac-illating to the opposite extreme. I saw myself in ministerial roles and positions that God had not directed for me. Then, I heard the Lord say, "Come away. Walk a few miles with me. Let your head clear. Let me change your heart. I want to show you the work that I have des-tined just for you to do." I found out that who I wanted to be was not the exact person that God wanted me to be.

> For we are His workmanship, created in Christ Jesus
> for good works, which God prepared beforehand so
> that we would walk in them.
>
> — Ephesians 2:10 (NASB 1995)

"Yes!" I believe I am whom I wanted to be. I always wanted to finish strong, to keep the faith, to and walk out of here someday with the crown Peter speaks about.

> And when the Chief Shepherd appears, you will
> receive the unfading crown of glory.
>
> — 1 Peter 5:4 (NASB 1995)

I have replaced what I did not become with the Person who has come. His name is Jesus.

"Sifting" means "to cause smaller particulars to pass through a 'sieve' so as to remove lumps from the finer particulars that may fall into the container below."

Momma had the art of sifting down to a "T!" On many mornings, she lifted me onto the wooden table in our small kitchen. She knew I loved to watch her make fresh bread. Her breadmaking was a gift for the entire family. She always initiated her art for baking fine biscuits around five o'clock each morning.

With the actions of cat on a hot tin roof, she reached for the flour "sifter" that contained a screen-wire base. Then, with one dip into the old flour barrel, she scooped the right amount of flour to make a big pan of light, fluffy, brown, "cat-head" biscuits. With a well-orchestrated rhythm of shaking and pounding the sides of the sifter, the tiny flour particles found their way into the large wooden mixing bowl. Next, Momma bumped the sifter on her apron-covered knee to quickly discharged the lumps of flour that refused to go through the sifter. The large lumps of flour wanted to put on a show and to jump up and down on the sifter, but Momma put them in their place. The place for the lumps was in the bucket of slop for the hogs where Momma unmercifully cast them.

Momma was not the only person who used a sifter to dump the clumps that appeared in their lives.

Job sifted through lumps of faulty accusations that were levied against him by Satan. Satan accused Job of serving God only because of God's blessings, but later, Job accused God of just buying Job's worship.

However, in the end, Job dumped Satan's lumps of faulty allegations in a volley of well-delivered discourses levied against his three friends and Satan.

Solomon sifted through lumps of rhetorical and religious intellectualism. His candid writings of discourses and treaties bring to light the writer's quandary with the vanities of life.

However, the wise man summed up life's journey after he had sifted through the obvious and the certainties. He simply made two observations: he said that the whole duty of man is to fear God and to keep his comments (see Ecclesiastes 12:13).

Elijah sifted through some very dark and dreadful lumps of psychological issues. He sat by a small brook and battled unhealthy thoughts of depression and individualism (1 Kings 19:4, 14), but the prophet of God shook off his self-imposed lumps with a final fiery display of God's favor (see 2 Kings 2:11).

Finally, we see the Apostle Paul, who sifted through the poisonous lumps of spiritual junk food and catchy opinions of his day that attempted to make his message of the cross both trite and nonapplicable (see 2 Timothy 4:3), but the Apostle triumphantly dumped all of the humanistic reasoning of his day onto the solid grounds of faith and resolve to finish his mission and to win a crown of life (see 2 Timothy 4:1-8).

So, what is left for me to say about the sifting process that took place in my life?

I finally acknowledged that I had allowed my reasoning, decision-making, leading and feeding my flock, and my own maturing process to be influenced by many unpalatable elements in my life. Demons they were, such as personal intimidation, peer jealousy, financial anxieties, and desiring to please everyone. Lumps they were! Those high-jumping attention-grabbers were never meant to be a part of my daily bread of life. So, I sifted them all from my life. The value of my personal walk with God increased by one hundred percent.

"Sometimes there is nothing else left to do but to walk away and go on with our lives." Those were the words that my Grandpa told his family on that dark, dismal day they decided to return to Arkansas.

Grandpa had purchased a ticket for the entire family to travel by train from White County, Arkansas, to Ocala, Florida, to work in the orange harvest, but Grandpa had another purpose for going to Florida. He wanted to plant a church in the fruit orchard community to reach the poor migrant workers who came to pick oranges. Grandpa believed that those precious people would receive the Word of God readily. He only wanted to pick oranges, but he also intended to pick souls for the kingdom of God.

Upon their arrival in Florida, a prominent farmer dropped by to welcome the family. He noticed that Grandpa's little children were somewhat undernourished. He insisted that Grandpa take "free of charge" one of the cows and "used the mile and butter for the little ones." Grandpa was ecstatic. He welcomed the gift of hospitality. Then, with a thankful heart, he gave thanks to God for His bountiful gift.

A few weeks later, another farmer dropped by who had been attending the prayer meetings that Grandpa had begun. He informed Grandpa that the farmer had spread malicious accusations throughout the community. "That preacher stole one of my milk cows and is using the mile and butter for himself."

Grandpa was crushed with grief and sorrow at the report. He promptly retuned the cow, offered apologies for the misunderstanding, and offered to pay for the milk and butter.

Consequently, his mission work was affected. It was too late for damage control to right the false accusations. The harm was too costly. So, Grandpa made the painful decision to pack up and to move back to Arkansas.

It was a long ride back home, and Grandpa and Grandmother sifted through the matter with tearful eyes. Why did God allow them to go to the orange harvest? Could God not have stopped the slander before it destroyed the church?

Then, they moved on and asked the Lord to direct the pathway that was before them.

As soon as the train crossed the Mississippi River, Grandpa noticed that it was harvest time in eastern Arkansas. The large cotton fields were begging to be picked. So, Grandpa found logging for the family and turned immediately to the harvest.

A few days passed. Then, one day, Grandpa looked up from the two rows of cotton that he picked. He stared into the face of a young man who led two mules through the cotton fields. They exchanged pleasantries, and then Grandpa introduced the young man to members of the family who worked alongside him. In the process of time, Grandpa heard the marriage vows of Raymond Black and Bessie Mitchell—my father and mother.

A few months passed. Grandpa received a telegram and a request for him to return to Florida as quickly as possible. The telegram was from the farmer who had spread the falsehoods against him earlier. The farmer asked for forgiveness. He also asked Grandpa to conduct his funeral. He stated he had only a few more hours to live.

That same year, Grandpa began a brush arbor revival among the cotton farm families. The brush arbor revival eventually gave birth to a strong church. A beautiful church building was later built. It became one of the prominent landmarks in that cotton town in eastern Arkansas.

Many years later, the mayor of the city where the church had been established asked me to perform his wedding. The ceremony was to be held in the beautiful church building that had its beginning in Grandpa's early ministry. While waiting in the large hallway to make my entrance, I spied a plaque with the names of all the former pastors. Marvin Monroe Mitchell, my Grandpa, was listed with others

R. Lloyd Black

who had served the church. Can you believe that for a moment my joy beamed with pride?

I began to tell my story in the beginning of this book with an account of my predecessors. I cited incidents, situations, and examples on how many of them walked on God's directed paths for their lives. Then, in each chapter, I shared how I connected with them with my own personal walk with God.

Now, as I close the last chapter of my story, I have one defining biblical reference that I would like to leave for others to share. It is a prayer that I choose to evoke upon me and my family. The Bible verses that comprise the prayer that I have chosen are as follows:

> May God, our very own God, continue to be with
> us just as he was with our ancestors—may he never
> give up and walk out on us. May he keep us centered
> and devoted to him, following the life path he has
> cleared, watching the signposts, walking at the pace
> and rhythms he laid down for our ancestors.
>
> — 1 Kings 8:57-58 (MSG)

SUMMARY AND APPLICATION

In a stuffy classroom where multiple grades were taught by one saintly lady, my life was influenced by the teacher. On a twenty-acre cotton sharecrop farm in eastern Arkansas that laid buried under gumbo, weeds and grass, my life was impelled by the hardships of life and the simplicity of survival, and in a small rural Church of God with scarcely enough people to wash the saints' feet, my soul was inspired to become a Pentecostal preacher.

The school, the field, and the church defined me, directed me, and developed me to be whom God intended for me to be. Within those three groups of character catalysts, God provided me with "tidbits" of educational appreciation, religious participation, and hard work application to chisel out His niche in life for me.

Then, God filled me with His Spirit and set my feet to dancing and my hands to clapping.

I was glad to be included in the household of faith and the kingdom of God.

I cannot look back at the old schoolhouse, because it was torn down a half century ago. I cannot work another long and hot day in that old cotton field, because it now produces rice, soybeans, and milo. Neither can I kneel just one more time at the old dusty altar in that little white-framed country Pentecostal church.

However, I can thank God for the journey. He directed my pathway, and I can praise Him for the voice that called me; the hand that protected me!

A few days ago, I took perhaps my last trip by to Woodruff Country. I saw approximately where Bear Slough used to be. Heavy equipment had removed the vegetation and mammoth trees and had filled the shallow water channel. The whole area was now leveled to ensure the proper flow of the irrigational system that popularized that aspect of farming.

I wondered what happened to the "Red Bird." I looked at the place where its favorite tree used to be. I'm sure it would have been surprised to have learned just what had happened to the boy at the other end of the fishing pole.

I long to share its influence on my life.

As I drove down the paved road that used to be the road less-graveled, I envisioned two bare feet, a straw hat and a ten-year-old boy who made countless journeys along that pathway.

R. Lloyd Black

Then, I paused for one last look at the small plot of ground that used to be my Daddy's twenty acre sharecrop. Here is where I learned about God's seed time and harvest:

"Sowing seed is sure need be,
if a farmer is gonna survive,
Every year, as spring appears,
his world seems to come alive.
He plants a tiny seed of cotton
And that seed, well it's gotta die,

If the farmer stands a chance,
to put a little money in his pants.

By the coming of winter time
He digs the dirt until it hurts
And then he watches the ground
As plant comes through
To tell the truth, God takes over now

That seedling appears, and then takes root.
So it can bear the wind and weight of the fruit.

Then a stalk, some leaves, and because of prayer,
next, he sees a tiny square.

A pinhead, a matchhead, a tiny candle!
God's doing it all, 'cept holding the hoe handle.

It's white, then pink, and the third day red,
Reminds the farmer of his Savior, so he bows his
head

Gives his thanks, for all he sees,
And what he didn't, like harmful disease.

He knows that crop was multiplied, by the Almighty
And then a battle was raging and the devil was
fighting.

He brought on drought, but God brought a rain.
Satan sent bugs, but then a strong wind came.

The faith of the farmer, prayer in Jesus' Name,
Made this crop his best ever.

So, this testimony he gave,
Just like the seeds, so are the souls.
We all have our choices, in His Word that is told.

We must die to self, before we can live.
And the stages of life, at times we get, then we give.

If we want others' souls, to come to the kingdom,
We must let God raise us so that everyone can see
Him.

From our praying to our staying with our spouses
always,
Forgiving and living with hearts full of praise.

That cotton and me ain't different at all,
I pray my roots, don't let my fruit fall.

God is so good and He's faithful, too.
You see, He's the Soul Farmer,
Tak'n care of me and you!" [2]

R. Lloyd Black

"I will arise and go now,
For always night and day...
While I stand on the roadway,
Or on the pavements gray..." [3]

- List discoveries you made when you sifted through
  your own past events, relationships, and persons. How
  did you react to them today? When Jesus prayed in the
  garden on the eve of his betrayal, what were the major
  thoughts that were on His mind? See John 17.

- How would you define "sifting?" List the causes and
  effects of hurtful situations or circumstances in your
  past. Have you been able to dismiss them from your
  present thoughts? How did Paul react to his adversities?
  See Acts 20:19-20.

- What was the greatest aspect of surprise you discovered
  about yourself when you sifted through past feelings and
  emotions?

EPILOGUE

Perhaps you have finished reading God's Directed Paths and now you know my story. You may even ask the question, "Is it possible that God has directed my path?"

To answer your question, I would suggest your reading and meditating upon several Bible verses. These Bible references lend themselves to that very possibility. I personally like Proverbs 20:24 (MSG), where the writer says, "The very steps we take come from God, otherwise how would we know where we're going?"

Even Shakespeare states that God intervenes in our personal life: "There is a divinity that shapes our ends, rough-hew them how we will.

I have always been intrigued by the life of Jacob. Jacob is an Old Testament Bible character. His life is long-playing. You can learn about Jacob by reading Genesis chapters 25-49.

The most fascinating aspects of Jacob's life is the role God plays. God spoke about Jacob's journey before Jacob was born (Genesis 25:23). Incredible! Yet, God allowed Jacob to live the life that he chose, and Jacob chose a life checkered with conflicts of deceit, rebellion, fears, and flight.

When I read the story of Jacob, I see him always running. He runs from the wrath of his brother and the wrath of his uncle. He runs from Canaan, and he runs from Haran. He runs from conflicts in family relationships and he runs from social relationships.

He certainly would have made an excellent long-distance track star.

However, Jacob could not run from himself, and he could not run from God. God always appeared on Jacob's pathway at Jacob's most critical need of the Lord.

Jacob's story ends well. You just have to wait for the story to end. As he laid dying, Jacob instructed his family members to take his body out of Egypt and to bury it in the land of Canaan. Canaan had been given to Jacob by the Lord during Jacob's most fearful and dark hour (Genesis 28:13).

What is so beautiful and amazing about the story Jacob is his resolve to hold onto God's promise regardless of his suffering in his lifetime.

> "Perhaps we have a spiritual lesson here as well: not only does the believer's spirit go to heaven when he or she dies, but the body will also be taken from this world at the resurrection."
>
> — Warren Wiersbe

I like the way that the writer of Hebrews sums up Jacob's long and lustrous life: "By faith Jacob, when he was dying, blessed each of the sons of Joseph, and worshiped, leaning on the top of his staff" (Hebrews 11:21, NKJV).

> "God did not choose Jacob because of who he was; God chose Jacob because of who he could become."
>
> — Unknown

What about you? Perhaps you suffer from a broken heart or from your fears of your past. It's possible that you may even feel that God has walked out on you, but God's Word declares differently. The Word says that God is with you throughout your entire journey of life.

> And who would dare tangle with God by messing with one of God's chosen? Who would dare even to point a finger? The One who died for us—who raised to life for us! —is the presence of God at this very moment sticking up for us. Do you think anyone is going to be able to drive a wedge between

us and Christ's love for us? There is no way! Not trouble, not hard times, not hatred not hunger, not homelessness, not bullying threats, not backstabbing, not even the worst sins listed in Scripture: They kill us in cold blood because they hate you. We're sitting ducks; they pick us off one by one. None of this fazes us because Jesus love us. I'm absolutely convinced that nothing—nothing living or dead, angelic or demonic, today or tomorrow, high or low, thinkable or unthinkable—absolutely nothing can get between us and God's love because of the way that Jesus our Master has embraced us.

— Romans 8:33-39 (MSG)

APPLICATION

Now that I have shared with you that God knows the path you will take in life and that God will never walk away from you, consider this challenge:

- Take sheet of paper and write down four words: Suffering, Searching, Serving, Sifting.

- Take your Bible and your thoughts and begin to journalize your own walk of suffering.

- Just jot down those events of suffering that painfully come to mind.

- With every situation that surfaces, write a Bible verse beside that dreadful moment.

Example: you recall a story that circulated that pitted you wrongfully or unfairly. Perhaps the story was financially costly. It could have showered great grief upon you and your entire family. Take heart. God has a Word for you on how He deals with that kind of stuff:

> Don't panic. I'm with you. There's no need to fear for I'm your God. I'll give you strength. I'll help you. I'll hold you steady, keep a firm grip on you. "Count on it. Everyone who had it in for you will end up out in the cold—real losers. Those who worked against you will end up empty-handed—noting to show for their lives. When you go out looking for your old adversaries you won't find them—Not a trace of our old enemies, not even a memory. That's right. Because I, your God, have a firm grip on you and I'm not letting go. I'm telling you, 'Don't panic, I'm right here to help you.'
>
> — Isaiah 41:10-13 (MSG)

- Now, work through the other three aspects of your life: Searching, Serving, and Sifting. Journalize the memories for each of those categories. Then, place a Bible reference with a promise alongside each situation, circumstance, or catastrophe.

POSTSCRIPT

Before I sign off, allow me to give some concluding thoughts about the dream that initially had at the age eighteen. You may remember I admitted that I struggled with the meaning of the dream. I saw people as though they were waters, the "falling of the Holy Spirit" as waves of glory, and my helplessness to speak.

In the past, I struggled to force certain events or situations in my ministry to make it fit the scenario of my dream. My intent was to fulfill my dream and to bring closure to it.

For example, there was a time that I ministered to a small group of service personnel and a handful of islanders on the banks of a Pacific island. We had no permanent building to shelter the flock and we met in the open air, but it gave me great opportunities to meet various ethnic groups who readily used the beautiful ocean beach.

During that pastoral period, I also taught college English to finance my ministry. My classes were packed with teenagers who spoke diversified languages and dialects. The student body was a large hodgepodge of multi-cultures. With God's help, I was able to introduce Christ to a few of the students. Maybe, I reasoned, this is the fulfillment of the dream that I had about people and the ocean.

Then came the period of time when I published several books. The books targeted rural church administration and growth principles. Some of the books were distributed to pastors and churches in both English and Spanish settings. I could see how the books would speak when I was unable to converse. Is this the fulfillment of my dream? I wondered.

Then, at the close of my pastoral ministries, I experienced my greatest fulfillment and growth in pastoral leadership. I had been assigned to lead a metropolitan city church. After a few years of maintenance ministry with old ideas and outdated ministry formats, the new arrived. God sent people from the Black American neighborhoods,

Kenya, Sierra Leone, Cameroon, Nigeria, Korea, Mexico, Nicaragua, the Bahamas, Haiti, and Jamaica to grow their indigenous ministries in the shelter of our church. These precious saints, in turn, added great value and fellowship to the old lethargic church community I had inherited. We soon became one church—but with many languages.

Finally, I mused, *This is the fulfillment of my Holy Spirit dream.*

However, truthfully, I was never satisfied with my attempts to fulfill my dream with my own logic. My spirit was just not buying into my explanations.

After all, I reasoned, *I must obey the commandments of Proverbs 3:5 (KJV):* "…Lean not unto thine own understanding."

So, now I ask myself a diagnostic question!

Do I believe that the dream that I wrote about is for an appointed time? Who knows!

Do I believe that it has a spiritual significance? Perhaps.

While I cannot offer a fitting interpretation to the dream, I would like to share a closing possibility about what I saw.

The Bible tells us that a mighty Holy Ghost revival is ongoing and will continue to the end of the age. Here are some references: Joel 2:29-32 and Acts 2.

While Joel spoke about the outpouring of the Spirit hundreds of years before Peter preached on the Day of Pentecost, Peter gave additional light to Joel's prophecy. Peter said that the presence of the Spirit on the Day of Pentecost was the same Spirit that Joel had spoken about, but Peter did not say that it was the fulfillment of the prophecy. Peter goes on and says that God will continue to call others and to baptize them in the Spirit (see Acts 2:38-39). This gives me hope that my children and my children's children are also included in the act of God.

However, some believe that the good times have all passed. They counter that we are now faced with just the bad times.

I certainly agree that the bad times are definitely upon us. I further believe that these horrible days that we are now experiencing will certainly increase and get considerably darker as we wait for the coming of Christ.

Here are some Bible references that point to the dark and death-oriented times and events that are still yet to come:

- 2 Timothy 2
- 2 Timothy 4:3-5
- 2 Peter 3
- Jude 17-19

"But can we have both the continuous outpouring of the Spirit at the same time that we are having an increase in sin and immorality?" you may ask. "Are we to conclude that the Bible is ambivalent?"

My answer to that questions is, "No, the Bible is not ambivalent!" It never contradicts itself.

Both the good times and the bad times are now upon us, and both the good times and the bad times will continue right up to the coming of Jesus to rapture the church.

————————

The phrase "both the good times and the bad times" remind me of the words of Charles Dickens. He said:

> "It was the best of times, it was the worst of times, it was the age of wisdom, it was the age of foolishness, it was the epoch of belief, it was the epoch of incredulity, it was the season of light, it was the season of darkness, it was the spring of hope, it was the winter of despair."

Like, Dickens, I conclude that this is the finest hour ever for the body of Christ, but it is also the darkest hour for the world.

The number one reason why I believe that it is the finest hour for the church is because God always chooses to act for His people in the darkest of hours. For example:

- God moved in creation in the dark hour and brought light (Genesis 1:3).

- God told Noah to build an ark when the earth was filled the darkness of sin and immorality (Genesis 6:13-14).

- God called Abram from the dark, modern, pagan world of Chaldees (Genesis 12:1).

- God heard the cry of the Israelites in Egypt's darkness (Exodus 2:7-10).

- God called Samuel when darkness invaded the temple (1 Samuel 3:1-3).

- God called Isaiah after national distress plunged the state into darkness (Isaiah 6:1-9).

- God spoke to Zacharias after four hundred years of dark silence (Luke 1:13-20).

- God called Saul to minister when the early church experienced its darkest hour (Acts 9).

Even Jesus, our Lord and Savior, appears in history in Capernaum to act in mercy and grace in the dark hour.

He brings light, miracles, and healings to the landscape that had been decimated with death, disease, despair, and darkness.

That it might be fulfilled which was spoken by Esaias the prophet, saying:

> The land of Zebulon and the land of Naphthalin,
> by the way of the sea, beyond Jordan, Galilee of

the Gentiles; The people which sat in darkness saw great light; and to them which sat in the region and shadow of death light is sprung up.

— Matthew 4:14-16 (KJV)

So, let me bring this thought to full circle and apply an application to this discourse if possible.

As I write, the COVID-19 virus appears to reign supreme over the entire planet. The virus has swept every nation, kindred, and tongue. It has invaded every workplace, homeplace, and safe place. No mountain top, low valley, province, village, island, desert, or metropolis are able to flee from its venomous wrath. It attacks unmercifully the children, the youth, and the elderly. The elite, poor, educated, and the uneducated have each been stricken by its traumatic assault. Likewise, the politicians, professionals, preachers, movie stars and musicians, sport figures, have been stung by this killer virus bee. Yes. This is indeed a very dark hour for all of mankind.

It looks like COVID-19 has won! It's such a dark hour educationally, financially, and socially. Little struggling churches lay scattered across the entire world.

However, God sees the darkness, and God has a track record of acting in power in the dark hour.

In the dark hour, God may choose to penetrate the ends of the earth, to pour out His Spirit abundantly, to bring healings and times of refreshing unprecedently to the entire planet.

And with the blast of Your nostrils The waters were gathered together; The floods stood upright like a heap; The depths congealed in the heart of the sea.

— Exodus 15:8 (NKJV)

In the dark hour, God acts for His people in a well-defined manner. God acts alone. He acts sovereignly! He needs no well-orchestrated theological schemes. He needs no new light from charismatic teachers. He needs no hastily-prepared prophetic utterances spoken by some impatient mass media motivational speaker. God acts alone—for His people!

What I see today through the darkness of the pandemic curse is my God acting in this very moment for His people.

First comes the outpouring of the virus; now we see God pouring out of His Spirit in the abundance of healings and Holy Ghost baptizing.

Great things ahead!

About the Author

R. Lloyd Black has served in Christian ministries for over six decades. He was born in 1941 on a twenty-acre sharecrop cotton farm in Woodruff Country, Arkansas.

Dr. Black earned his Bachelor of Science in Education and his Master of Science in Education from Arkansas State University. He received his Doctorate of Ministry Degree from Luther Rice Theological Seminary in 1981. He completed extensive postgraduate work at the Pentecostal Theological Seminary in Cleveland, Tennessee. He completed a Master's equivalency in Curriculum and Leadership Development in Secondary Education at UCA in Conway, Arkansas.

He taught English classes in high school and college for thirteen years. He served as seminary professor and business administrator for three years.

He began his preaching and teaching ministry in 1959 when he was issued and exhorter's permit. He was ordained in 1966. He also served as state youth director, pastor, national evangelist, and national conference speaker for several years.

Some of the books published by the author include *Holy Ghost and Speaking with Tongues*, *Every Member A Worker*, *Practical Pastoral Principles*, and *Yet Not I*. He also wrote Sunday school literature, booklets, and brochures for the evangelism and outreach department for his international church affiliate for several years.

Pastor Black has been married to Pat (Chandler) for fifty-eight years. Together, they have traveled and ministered throughout most of the United States, the Middle East, Europe, the Caribbean, and Pacific Islands.

They have two married children, Kimi and Ray Jr., four grandchildren, and two great grandchildren.

Lloyd and Pat are currently serving as pastors for the Danville, Arkansas Assembly of God church.

Endnotes

[1] Francis A. Mitchell, *An Old Soldier's Story, Recollections of My Grandfather*, n.d.

[2] Shawn O'Shields, 2020.

[3] William Butler Yeats, *The Lake Isle of Innisfree*, 1890.

CPSIA information can be obtained
at www.ICGtesting.com
Printed in the USA
LVHW010846090621
689685LV00004B/482

9 781637 691762